Holes in My

Pockets

The Rules of Holes

A Stress-Free Book of Financial Health, Wit, and

Wisdom

By Craig Stellpflug

ISBN: 9781797896793

Contents

Where Health and Finances Intersect

There is a good reason I published this book under *Health and Wellness*. This is because physical health is often bound hand-in-glove to financial health. While stress in general causes oxidative damage in the body at the cellular level, financial stress combines with other factors to also damage relationships, reputations, and self-esteem. It has been said that *money can't buy happiness,* and this is true. However, money resources do help reduce stress in relationships, help enable healthier food selections, and provide better self-care choices. This book, *Holes in My Pockets,* will help you identify areas where money just seems to leak out like coins finding their way through a literal hole in your own pocket.

I pen this book with much personal candor applied with a little tongue in cheek humor. If I had to name *"who"* is this book written to I'd have to admit that this work is as much of a reminder to myself as it is written for the financially challenged. ~ Enjoy!

♦ Introduction ♦

After once having had plenty of money and also having spent it all, I was left smarting from the sting of near bankruptcy. Back then, what I had lost through foolishness and a lack of knowledge, I now call "tuition" in the education of life. I paid a dear and high tuition for the lessons I received when I lost my proverbial shirt through "not-so-good" business dealings and a lack of personal financial discipline. Hopefully, some of the lessons I learned and convey through this writing will help you, the reader, steer clear of some of the same pitfalls and holes that may lie ahead of you.

To pay the price for your financial education in life, three choices exist:

1   Study at the feet of successful teachers and mentors

2   Watch and heed the mistakes and successes of others

3   Make all your own mistakes and pay your own tuition

Whether you have money or have none at all, financial holes

are cleverly devised traps into which anyone might stumble. Beware; the price for financial education can be very steep! Experience taught me that. But you can choose option 2 above and learn from my successes and failures. That way the tuition I paid for financial lessons in my life may afford you a fine, upstanding financial education to help you better steward monies and assets both now and in your future at a much lesser cost.

I have often heard that insanity is doing the same thing over and over again and each time somehow expecting a different result.

If you are buried in a financial hole, caught in a vicious cycle, circling the drain, or just plain high centered and spinning your wheels and can't get ahead financially, this book can offer you hope and maybe some new direction so you can develop a plan to change your financial circumstances—and your financial future.

Warning: This book is not about dispensing financial advice or making stock and investment tips, but rather, a book about personal experience mixed with stories and anecdotes dressed up with a little tongue-in-cheek humor and underpinned with some actual serious thoughts.

1 ♦ Stop Digging!

The first rule of holes is:

If you are in a hole, and the hole is getting deeper,

STOP DIGGING!!!

In other words:

If you are surrounded by debt, and that debt is growing, stop feeding the debt!

Clearly, in this *"I want it now"* world surrounding us, it is nearly impossible to say *"I'll buy it later when I can afford it"*. Or *"I really do not think I can afford this right now."* These words have become foreign to many of our ears.

The advertisers say (and I quote):

"There has never been a better time to buy", *"Make no payments until next year"*, *"No credit refused"*, *"Easy monthly payments"*, *"Buy now pay later"*, *"Your trade-in has never been worth more"*, *"You can't afford to miss this one"*, *"But wait, there's more, if you order now we will send you, absolutely free…"*, *"Have your credit card ready…"*

Take heed! If you are in a financial hole then anytime you hear one of these phrases, **stop, drop and roll!** Cover your ears and say in a loud voice, *"La-la-la-la-la, I can't hear you!"* What you just heard are some of the schmoozing slogans and promises made by virtually every credit lender and marketer vying for your credit gleanings. Innovative and proven consumer debt marketing strategies are relentlessly and aggressively scheming to capture your personal indebtedness as soon as possible, at the earliest legal age possible, and most definitely before the competition can catch you.

How often have you found yourself answering these seductive ads by saying; *"I just really cannot afford that right now"*, *"I think I'll save up and pay cash"*, or *"Let me see if this is really the best product with the best deal"*, or (my favorite) *"You know, I just realized that I never really used the last thingy-gizmo I bought"*!

I'm afraid that the usual answer we have to the lender and marketer's Sirenous songs will more often be... *"Wow, let me have one of those!"* *"They are right! I would be a fool to pass on this deal!"*, *"They're almost sold out??"*, *"You mean I can order it right now by phone and have it shipped today?"*, *"I'll be the first on my street to have one of them!"*, *"If I buy now, I'll receive absolutely free not one but three..."*.

Our minds are subconsciously reeling as we attempt to reason within ourselves: *"I really need this"*, *"I've got to have this"*, *"not only will it make me smarter, but I don't even know how I have survived this long without a counter top, high speed, state of the art, self-cleaning, auto pilot,* *twice reversing, thingy-gizmo with an oscillating aperture and burl walnut faux finish". "This will save me so much time", "It will reduce my weight", "make me thinner", "improve my looks **and** save me money on stuff I never used to buy before I got one of these coooool... uhm... whatchamacallits"...*

Alongside the impulse-inducing sales pitch, and ingenious and captivating infomercials, the eager marketers have their sculpted solution to your supposed problem of needing this or that when you cannot afford it now. CREDIT. You can own this today and pay for it tomorrow (plus tax, title, interest, carrying charges, and origination fees.) Then print gets smaller—Oh BTW, *and* shipping, handling *and* other incidental fees, cost, honorariums *and* other hidden charges may also apply... Just sign here please_____. In the real game of life, Peter's collection agency is right across the street from Paul's loan shop.

The Runaway Freight Train

A different way to state the first rule of holes is:

You have to stop a runaway freight train before you can back it up!

A runaway debt train is fierce to see. The heavier the cargo of debt, the further that old debt train will roll when you try to stop it. The law of inertia will keep it moving forward even under full emergency brakes and make it difficult and nearly impossible to stop without a devastating derailment.

To stop the old debt train from rolling any further you have several options:

Option 1: Stop borrowing

It takes intestinal fortitude to stay away from the easy finance and refinance traps. *Especially when the finances are tough and getting tougher.* In order to get out of any financial debt hole you absolutely have to stop borrowing. No question about it!

Option 2: Increase your income

Keep in mind that even if you increase your income, you still have to stop borrowing to stop the debt train, so at this point I'll refer you back to option 1.

(Bear in mind that devices and schemes to pay off debt that are planned and instituted while rapidly digging an even bigger debt hole are likely to end in train-wreck and/or bankruptcy. In fact, if you are still incurring more debt while trying to make more money to pay the more debt, the whole process will accelerate and the hole will start to dig itself.)

Option 3: Win the state lottery!

(But even if you do actually, somehow, against insurmountable odds, win the lottery and pay off your debts, you still have to remain debt free to stay out of the proverbial hole.)—Once again refer to option 1—*And now that*

I think about it, I have never seen or heard of a banking institute buying lottery tickets as an investment venture or taking the daily customer deposits to the boats for gambling. And why don't banks sell lottery tickets at the deposit counters if they are such good investments? I wonder...)

Option 4: See option 1

(But again, I repeat myself)

There are many ways to stop the damage incurred by financial holes *and* reverse the hole-digging *and* still pay your honest debts. But they all start by stopping. That is, stopping the debt growth of course.

I leave this chapter with a final word:

If you made a debt or borrowed money in good faith, it is an honest debt and you should pay it back in good faith—period, no arguments. After all, it is your personal word and your integrity that is at stake.

2 ♦ Change Something!

The second rule of holes is:

Nothing Changes if Nothing Changes!

As bad as you may want to change something in your life (like a financial future), until actions are taken in a different direction, everything will continue moving on the same trajectory without fail.

To illustrate this point: Have you ever encountered a Chinese finger trap? This is a woven tube just big enough for you to insert a finger into each of the ends. Once you insert the index finger of each hand into the trap it is impossible to pull your fingers back out. In fact, the harder you pull, the tighter the finger trap becomes! The weave of the finger trap binds smaller as you pull and stretch the trap in attempts to remove your fingers. As long as you keep pulling you will never get out of this conundrum. However, if you simply reverse the direction and push instead of pulling, the weave of the finger trap loosens up and you can push the finger trap off with ease.

A new direction will break the dynamics of any cycle.

In other words, debt traps are also like finger traps. The harder you pull the more they bind you. Reverse direction of motion and the conundrum solves itself.

Story number 1: *Amy and Ted's story*

Amy and Ted were living in the home of their dreams. The problem was that financial ruin was closing in on them fast. Late payments were hitting them first, then a bounced check along with the associated bank charges. The cycle was set and they were circling the drain. They originally purchased the house because of a juicy promotion at Ted's work that came with a substantial pay raise. A few months later, business cutbacks came to Ted's work. Then a large and unexpected car repair trounced upon them along with a personal emergency that sent them reeling into a financial crunch.

In order to break the dynamics of this pernicious cycle they first had to see and admit to the fact that they had prematurely jumped into the dream house they only *thought* they could afford. Rather than fighting to keep everything together and pay deferred payments on the house and charge the car repairs, they knew that they had to change their financial direction or keep digging an even bigger debt hole. Acting accordingly, they quickly sold the dream home and used the small bit of equity they managed to salvage to repair the car and cover the personal emergency charges with cash. After this they could also pay down on another "lesser" house that they could really afford.

In selling off the dream home they worked so hard for, they stove off the looming possibilities of embarrassing bankruptcy and also the probable and imminent loss of their home to foreclosure. In a new and stronger financial position (on the outside of the financial hole), they were able to manage and decrease their consumer debts, save *and invest* their money, **and** their once outrageously stressed lives were now much simpler. I am personally convinced that this also saved their marriage. They realized *before* it was too late that nothing changes if nothing changes.

A few short years later, after a few wise investments and keeping "the same old car" for 4 years longer than they originally planned to, they actually found an even better deal on a home that was comparable to their lost dream home.

The point to this story is that when they saw the direction they were headed and knew it was a bad one, Amy and Ted quickly made life-changing decisions to save their immediate, and their ultimate financial future. As a side bonus, both of them reported a better marital relationship with the pressure of finances off of their minds. The success they had in working together to cultivate their futures and triumph over the debt hole brought them closer together with common goals in a common battle.

The lack of finances increasing consumer debt and all the pressure thereof, is a major contributing factor in the alarming growth of divorce in the world today. Pulling together to fight the battle against a real enemy—like debt— can be both a rewarding experience and a huge relief from the insurmountable battles that couples often wrongly fight against each other.

While not everyone will have equity in their home in a situation like this, it is still better to cut losses and choose the remedy, rather than to have *the **end** choose the losses!*

Opt to sell off the house rather than suffer inevitable foreclosure after a long and damned struggle.

It's kinda like having a bald tire on the old family station wagon. You can change it at **your** convenience or eventually you **will** change it at your *in*-convenience. You choose the time and place or it chooses you.

If what you are doing today is not working... do something different tomorrow.

If that doesn't work tomorrow, then try something else again the next day.

Remember, nothing changes if nothing changes!

Story number 2: The man with the crooked handlebars

There once was a man whose sole transportation was a bicycle. The man rode it everywhere. It had a basket mounted over the front tire, flashing safety lights for nighttime biking, and a rear

17

fender that would keep the tire splash off of his back when it rained. The bike was about as unique as he was—but it also had crooked handlebars. It was really an odd sight to see him coming down the street with one hand on one side of the handlebar higher and closer to his body than the other side. It seemed to be his trademark.

Then one sunny day while he was working, his fellow employees decided to do him a huge favor and straighten the handlebars for him while he was busy and not looking. The well-intending co-workers thought that they were performing some great act of benevolence and took extra pains to get the alignment just right. They accomplished the repairs quickly and quietly during their break that day and waited in proud anticipation for his discovery of what they had done to bless him.

And now, what do you suppose happened? Well, rather than having you guess that he was overjoyed and fainted or became angry or some other thing, I'll tell you that the man didn't even notice the change made to his handlebars as he strapped his lunch pail into the basket. He hopped up on his bike with his usual adieus and he was off with a big wave good-bye, wobbled back and forth a bit and immediately crashed his bike straight into a telephone pole!

I suppose there are some wonderful morals to learn in this story about neighbors helping each other, meaning well, doing good always, and so on, but the point that I want to make is that this man was so acclimated to steering his bicycle with the crooked handlebars that he couldn't pilot the bicycle safely once the handlebars were straightened to what they should have been.

Here's the point: If you have been operating your finances a certain way and now you are adjusting the financial handle bar, *(because nothing changes if nothing changes)* there will be a new learning curve to be dealt with. There are adjustments in your brain's navigational system, so to speak, that have to kick in before you can comfortably steer correctly. So, don't be too surprised if when you make an adjustment to your crooked handlebars that you appear to steer straight for trouble until you get your new bearings. And for the love of Pete, if you have trouble adjusting to the new steering at first, do not re-realign the steering back to the original crookedness!

I've heard it said: The main difference between a rut and a grave is the dirt in your face.

So, if you are in that proverbial rut and your handlebars are crooked, make a change. Run the opposite direction, do something different. But remember to make allowances for the learning curve and figure in some adjustment time rather than falling back into the grave (er, I meant to say rut?) that you were in before.

When you make changes, it may take a while to adjust to them.

19

3 ♦ Rat Logic (Say Cheese!)

The third rules of holes is:

Even if you win the rat race, you're still a rat!

Why are you in the rat race if you're not a rat? The rat race is depicted by the exercise wheel that the rat gets on that goes around and around and goes nowhere, produces nothing. The wheel is an outlet, however, for pent up ambition. Without the wheel, the rat becomes restless, then lethargic, and then the rat dies an early death. Not good for the rat, huh? So then, if you want keep a rat healthy, get it a wheel to run on. If you are an enterprising individual, you might even harness the wheel to a generator or some machine that would produce marketable goods.

With all that said, I ask you, ARE YOU A RAT? If you *are* a rat, then you may want to use this book for nesting material. If you are *not* a rat then start looking for a lever to pry your cage open. Remember, a fox will gnaw his foot off to escape a trap and avoid the hunter. He would rather limp through life than become pelt fodder for some person's coat. Mankind on the other hand tries to get comfortable in their trap. *"Hey honey, bring me a beer and the TV remote, I'm stuck in this trap and need entertainment. I'm gonna be here awhile so I might as well get comfortable."* The good news is that if you have to chew off your financial foot to get out of a trap, you can still regrow another one.

It was the Roman satirical poet Juvenal (circa A.D. 100) that said in effect: "If you feed and entertain the masses, you can control them."

Rat-sense point one:

Rats are remarkable creatures to me—uh, tame varieties of course. Children (and even adults) actually enjoy sitting and watching a rat run on the ol' exercise wheel for long periods of time; running on and on and on but getting nowhere. Some exercise wheels can even be harnessed to generators, allowing the rat to charge batteries and run lights. The fact is that a healthy rat can run up to 27 miles in one day. A rat on a running wheel equipped with a generator can actually generate up to 500 milliwatts of electric power daily[1]. (A typical laser pointer outputs about five milliwatts of light power and a typical hearing aid for people operates on less than 1 milliwatt).

In order to keep a captive rat healthy, they absolutely have to have exercise. To accomplish this, an exercise wheel is the obvious choice of smart rat owners. So, why not have the rat

---

[1] Sherwin, C.M., 1998, Voluntary wheel running: A review and novel interpretation, Animal Behaviour, 56: 11–27

produce something while it is exercising? And this is where our point one analogy gels: Smart people know they have to work to stay financially healthy. Smarter people give the smart people an "exercise wheel" to run on that generates income for themselves—gleaned off the running wheel efforts of others.

Are you the rat on the exercise wheel?

Rat-sense point two:

The main reason researchers use rats for medical trials is because their brain and gut neurochemicals are actually closer to human than that of Rhesus monkeys. Rats also reproduce rapidly enough to provide generations of study input within just a few months. The fact is that a single pair of rats can produce as many as 2,000 descendants in just one year if left to breed unchecked[2].

Meanwhile a serious researcher controls the environment for their study subjects while they design and weight the trial to prove a presupposition (hypothesis). Because rats are fairly cheap and easy to come by, if the trial is going south and not bringing the desired results, dump the rats and start over! Once the researcher has tweaked, tuned (and sometimes twisted) the environmental

---

[2]Lentini, Liza, and David Mouzon. "20 Things You Didn't Know About Rats." Discover Magazine, 7 Dec. 2006, discovermagazine.com/2006/dec/10-things-rats. (Accessed online February 23, 2019).

variables in a study, they can manipulate outcomes to provide almost any study results they want[3].

Are you just another wheel in the cog of someone else's master social and financial design?

Rat-sense point three:

Being highly trainable, rats also tend to be creatures of habit. This is the main reason scientists employ rats for maze tests. Once a rat defeats a maze to capture the cheese, the scientist will move the cheese, change the environmental or other conditions and then record the results. Scientists know almost everything that makes a rat happy, fearful, healthy, more productive, sad, more social, antisocial and etc.

In fact, rats have been used in experimental mazes for over 100 years. Thousands upon thousands of studies have examined how rats run different types of mazes to study health parameters, spatial learning and memory capacity in rats. Maze studies help uncover general principles about learning, chemical, food, drug, emotional, and many other input results for rat studies that can be directly applied to humans.

Is someone moving your cheese and changing your maze?

---

[3] Every-Palmer, S. and Howick, J. (2014), EBM fails due to biased trials and selective publication. J Eval Clin Pract, 20: 908-914. doi:10.1111/jep.12147. (Accessed February 23, 2019)

Rat-sense point four:

Rats are both social and competitive creatures. Limited resources always result in competition among rats (and humans). Nevertheless, social animals (like rats or humans) also still retain innate preferences for cooperative behavior. In food-deprived rat studies, rats are found to display reciprocity while traveling and foraging together and even sharing limited resources. However, regardless of whether there is an abundance of resources or a lack thereof, there is always a race to the bait in every rat study. This competition produces social classes of clear leaders and ranking followers.[4] After all, someone has to get to the cheese first.

Interestingly, in studies, rats do not split up to collect the baits independently, but mostly travel together with leaders arriving first and followers after. Does this sound like a human condition?

The second rat gets the cheese

Before we move on, I would like to belabor one last rat-point. That is the fact that *the second rat to a rat trap gets the cheese!* The first rat to the bait gets his bell rung rather permanently and the second rat absconds with the prize. I've seen this happen quite often with inventors and entrepreneurs. The idea comes into

---

[4] Hoshaw, Brian A et al. "Social competition in rats: cell proliferation and behavior" *Behavioural brain research* vol. 175,2 (2006): 343-51.

fruition and the second rat comes by and scoops the idea and either buys it up for pennies or outright swipes it and runs to the patent office with as many ID changes to the idea as it takes to be the not-so-original but first patent holder and money recipient. When the actual first rat comes by, he is hammered mercilessly by the second rat. That's just how life is in the proverbial rat race. The question remains:

Why are you even in the rat race if you are not a rat?

4 ♦ The Neighborhood Competition

The fourth rule of holes is:

You'll never truly keep up with the Joneses

Just as the handlebars on your bicycle should be aligned for safe cycling, needs and wants absolutely have to be aligned to keep a balance in both life and in life's financial budget. For instance: I have seen people who have a tremendous need for something in their life and yet have little or no want to do what it takes to meet that need. Juxtaposed to that, I have seen even more of the kind of situation where there is a tremendous want—even an over desire (lust)—but no real need for the object of desire.

If you really want something but absolutely do not need it, this could be your first clue that you really should not get it. (Keep in mind that every individual has a different needs-to-wants ratio and there is no definitive benchmark in society to judge someone's situation by.)

Have you ever heard this saying?

"He who dies with the most toys, wins the game"?

Or should it actually read:

"He who dies with the most toys, still dies!"

All this to say: You should never judge yourself by what your neighbor has or what you have that he or she doesn't have. To accomplish this fete of non-judgement you will need both a strong self-identity and self-worth. A strong self-identity will not necessitate the accumulation of toys to remain intact. A weak self-identity has to be constantly propped up with inanimate things and external appearances to keep it from floundering in its shifting sands. Also, in my humble opinion, true self-worth should never be predicated upon physical possessions or appearances, but rather on personal moral standards and actions.

An essay on self-identity

The Oxford dictionary defines "self-identity" as: "The recognition of one's potential and qualities as an individual, especially in relation to social context".[5]

---

[5] "Self-Identity | Definition of Self-Identity in US English by Oxford Dictionaries." *Oxford Dictionaries | English*, Oxford Dictionaries, en.oxforddictionaries.com/definition/us/self-identity. (Accessed online February 23, 2019).

I would diverge from the textbook definition somewhat to say that your self-identity should not be so much about social context as about personal core values and how they shape your behavior within social context.

Who you think you are is, of course, a large part of your self-identity; that is, the way you look at yourself along with the core values you subsequently engage with the world around you. Understanding what self-identity is really about allows you to examine who you are, and perhaps more importantly, define, mold, develop and create who you ultimately want to be.

On a side note, self-identity is not to be confused with self-esteem. Self-esteem is your overall appraisal of personal worth at any single point in time—an emotional measurement, if you will, of how well you are living up to your own world views and core values. To cop to the idea of having to *"keep up with the Joneses"* is perhaps more of a self-esteem issue than anything else.

Now, if you mistakenly coin your self-identity to your nationality, career, family status, financial status, political/social status, or perhaps even your health status ("my asthma", "my cancer", "my muscular body", "my wealth"), then you are more likely than not setting yourself up for eventual failure when any of these statī change. This is what causes the old fashioned "identity-crisis".

Always keep in mind that social status is often a fragile position at best and higher social status positions are likely fleeting and easy to tumble from. In fact, to ascend to a certain "social class" of living and friends and pumped up self-esteem, and then to fall from the haute social graces would be devastating for a person who attempts to build their self-identity around a social status. A strong self-identity outside of social class, outward appearances, and material things is a must to combat this fifth rule of holes.

Sometimes our sense of self-identity is what keeps us in a hole.

Knowing who you really are with a healthy and strong self-identity will help you to condemn any hole/trap that prowls about to captivate you into debt while trying to gain and maintain a social status, outward appearances, and material things. In life, possessions and circumstances appear, disappear, and reappear for many reasons, but your true, authentic, deep core values rooted in self-identity should remain intact to help provide a stable foundation to continue living from.

As the mouth confesses so becomes the heart...

Some examples of confessions of a positive, healthy sense of self-identity outside of social standards could be:

I am witty and strong

I always tell the truth

I have a great sense of humor and compassion

I love to do good things for people without their knowledge

Kids are my passion

I love to teach people new things

I am a rock of support for people in need

Music and art stimulate me

I am sad when I see someone lose in life

Spring is always my favorite time of year

I am the type of person who has to be coddling the new baby

Crowds bother me but I hum my favorite song to distract myself

Bad examples of sense of self-identity might include:

Look at the car I drive and the house I live in!

Don't mess with me because my dad is a _____

Nobody hires _____ people like me

I'll remember what you did to me when I become rich/famous someday

I knew a lady whose sole sense of self and identity was her babies. When her babies eventually grew up, she became very insecure and even mentally unstable. People who identified themselves by their wealth jumped to their death in the stock-market crash of the 1920's. People who strive to keep up with the Joneses often finance the very trophies symbolizing their success to their own financial hurt.

In the competition with keeping up with the Joneses, you do not win trophies... you have to buy them!

A person with a strong identity of self and good balance of needs and wants will show it in their conversations, daily living, family life, and in their financial life.

5 ♦ Champagne Tastes

The fifth rule of holes is:

Never buy champagne on a beer budget

Everyone would like to think they have a connoisseur's taste for the finer things in life—Caviar, Cognac, Champagne, Cadillacs, and etc. While there is nothing wrong with having the finer things in life, there is always a bill that comes with every fine dining experience. Also, not only does the new Cadillac cost a gob of money outright, but even the monthly insurance bill alone can be more than the monthly payment on a lesser vehicle!

While I personally love a fine dining experience in an exotic place, I do not like the payments on a credit card that accrues monthly charges and interest. Given the choice then, if I cannot afford the cash outlay for my champagne tastes, I personally choose to enjoy the lesser dining experience of local cuisine. This happens when I keep myself within the parameters of a budget where I do not allow myself to spend extravagantly or buy on credit. So, even though I have champagne tastes, if I cannot afford the cash, I limit myself to the affordable beer budget.

Oh, I wish that I had a nickel for every time I heard someone say, "I wish I had all the money I spent on this or that thing".

Hindsight is, after all, 20/20 they say. This means that if you cannot see clearly what is coming up, you will definitely see it clearly *after* it hits you in the crosswalk of life.

A word to the wise...If you think you may ever be in the position to say "I wish I had the money I spent on..." DON'T SPEND IT! Take a long moment (or a week or month) to reflect on all the possibilities before you blow the cash (or worse yet, the credit). Driving impulse buying is what American advertising is all about.[6] A good test for determining an impulse buy is...*wait for it*...waiting a few days to see if the urge to buy subsides. It is almost never wrong to want better things than what you have now, it is often merely a matter of timing—and, of course, answering this question: "Can I afford this today"?

You see, our collective desires, and even lust, for improvements and conveniences helps drive capitalism. (This is especially true for the "baby boomers" who are hooked on conveniences.[7]) A gripping case of the "I want it now's" is what causes consumers to generate the bulk of consumer debt that

[6] Hartney, Elizabeth. "Don't Be Manipulated Into Overspending Due to Advertising." *Verywell Mind*, Dotdash, 21 Sept. 2018, www.verywellmind.com/five-advertising-tricks-that-trigger-impulse-buying-22229. (Accessed online February 23, 2019).

[7] Partners, WD. "Boomers Say Convenience Is King, Millennials Focus on Self Identity - What's a Brand to Do?" *PR Newswire: News Distribution, Targeting and Monitoring*, 18 Oct. 2012, www.prnewswire.com/news-releases/boomers-say-convenience-is-king-millennials-focus-on-self-identity---whats-a-brand-to-do-174765341.html. (Accessed online February 23, 2019).

they owe. Therefore: If you have a burning deep inside to have and to hold something right now—at any cost—it is probably something you *should not* have right now. That "burning" has to be checked and perhaps double-checked to make sure that whatever you are "burning" for on the inside, to have and to hold today, isn't just a passing fancy but indeed a lust.

I consider a lust to be an over-desire for something that isn't yours and is probably wrong for you to have right then.
A lust is usually accompanied by an overbearing, burning desire kind of feeling.

Case in point: *Don't drive a car that is more expensive than you can afford.*

Sherrie's story:

A friend and mentee of mine had a wonderful, older, paid off vehicle, but she really wanted a nice new convertible. However, the meager trade-in value of her used car was going to leave a whole lot of new car to be paid for with financing. She test-drove the new car by my house with the zeal of a 16-year-old sporting around in a new convertible. (She was a single mom in her 30's with a 5-year-old child at the time.) I assumed she was looking for my reaction while desiring my approval so I naturally asked her how was she going to pay for this shiny money-trap. She replied that she just started a sales position with an Internet company and would soon be making hundreds of extra dollars a week. And after all, she needed to show people that she was a success in her business by driving a vehicle that would match the success.

From my perspective, I suspected that the proverbial cart was being placed squarely in front of the horse in Sherrie's case. My advice to her was to make the new car a reward trophy she could obtain when her success proved out. She tossed these words back at me by stating her conviction: "I am confessing the fact that I am successful by driving a car like other successful people drive in this business". Do you know how hard it is to argue with someone's convictions?

I told her that her confession of faith was sincere enough, but she still did not have the CIF (cash in fist) yet. Sherrie pouted and fussed and I thought I might actually lose my friendship with her over this. In the end she decided to "appease me" and wait one month—just because I told her I thought it was an impulse buy. In the weeks that followed, she discovered that she wasn't the overnight superstar salesperson she thought she was. She was *pretty ok* at it though, and became moderately successful rather quickly. But the money did not really begin to flow for her for almost 8 months!

In retrospect she saw how she would have struggled to make new car and insurance payments right away, which would have also challenged her resolve for success with a financial defeat along with the accompanying negative attitude. At 8 months into her job she wisely made it her "success goal" to have 1 year of insurance prepaid and 3 months of loan payments saved ahead before she financed her shiny trophy. When she met her goal, the car truly became a symbol of her well-earned success and this jazzed her work success even more.

Remember back to the champagne taste and the beer budget thing? It is wiser to drive a cheaper car and save the payments that may max out your debt ratio.

"Pride goeth before the fall." sayeth the wise man.
"It is better to keep and drive a cheaper and older car than to lose a fancier car in the sight of your neighbors."

Try this on for size: When you think you are ready to buy a new car (or new _____), and you are determined to finance it, try putting the proposed payments aside for a year, then sell your old car (or old _____), and the buy your new car (or new _____) with a bigger down payment, more equity, and less interest payments. This will also help prevent you from being "upside down" on your new car deal (or new _____ deal) throughout the loan.

"Upside down" is where the balance you owe is more than what you can sell the once-new car for (or once-new _____ for). When this happens, you are stuck with your new car payments (or new _____ payments) and have no real way out of the deal without paying it completely off or suffering an embarrassing default. Having real equity in a vehicle once saved me a lot of trouble at a time when my income changed suddenly and I had to sell the vehicle. I actually got rid of a major expense payment and also had some cash back that helped me out in my time of trouble. Unfortunately, I later had another vehicle that I owed more than it was worth and suffered a costly repossession. If I had adhered to what I am saying now (remember that hindsight is 20/20), in retrospect I could have avoided some major hickeys on my credit report.

You do not want to live beyond your <u>means</u>. *Because that* <u>means</u> *that you could lose your* <u>means</u> *of transportation!*

Or as they say in the used car business:

"the quickest way to get back on your feet is to miss a payment".

This same beer budget principle applies to housing, furnishings, clothing, jewelry—and champagne.

6 ♦ How to Straighten a Bent Flagpole

The sixth rule of holes:

The key to your income is your outgo

A quaint little primary school in a rural community had a wonderful flagpole that stood proudly at the entrance of the school's driveway. It was tall and shiny with a bronze eagle fastened to the top of it. It was a great flagpole and "Old Glory" was a really fine sight to see displayed so perfectly in front of the classic school buildings and symmetrical driveway. The school's maintenance man took great care to keep the paint fresh, the ropes clean and white and the flag untangled at all times.

Then one cloudless day an unexpected storm front blew through with a huge wind and a gust that bent the flagpole before anyone could lower the flag. It wasn't that bad of a bend but it was noticeable. The cost of a new pole was quite a bit and the maintenance man thought he could save the school some money if he could just straighten out the old pole. So, he tied one end of a thick rope to the top of the pole and tied the other end to a come-a-long at the base of a tree that was away from the bend in the flagpole. His idea was to pull the pole straight with the leverage of the come-a-long. He then tightened up the rope click by click until the pole stood exactly straight again. But alas, whenever he let the tension off of the rope, the pole went back to the same old bend again!

Well, needless to say, the maintenance man was quite flustered with this sad turn of events. He was just standing there, a-scratching his head and studying the situation out as an old man came walking by. The old man, seeing the perplexed look on the maintenance man's face, asked him what was the trouble. The maintenance man explained that even though he pulled the pole to a straight position, when he let go of the tension the pole always returned to its original position. The old man laughed and said, *"I guess you didn't know that in order to straighten out a bent flagpole you have to bend it just as far back in the opposite direction."* Seeing the wisdom in this advice, the maintenance man stretched the rope one more time with the come-a-long. This time though, he pulled the flagpole all the way past center and back toward the tree. When he relieved the tension off of the flagpole this time it returned to dead center.

The moral of this story is: *to straighten a bent flagpole you have to bend it back in the opposite direction.*

If your finances are the bent flagpole then the measures that you have to take to straighten them out will require bending the flagpole in the opposite direction. You will have to make sacrifices (like Ted and Amy's story in chapter 2) and change the direction from borrowing to not borrowing **and** you will have to aggressively attack that debt to resolve it *(make your flagpole stand perfectly straight)*.

The key to your income is often your outgo!

If your flagpole is bent severely toward the spending direction you will have make a coarse correction and bend it back all the way in the other direction—and then some. Stop spending so much! Counter-steer in the other direction. Start watching the dimes and where they go and the dollars will take care of themselves.

In our lives, we occasion upon what I would call people of influence. People who we respect that influence us by their lifestyle, demeanor, and even their words. These remarkable people mentor us from time to time with little one-liners that sometimes sit in our thoughts for days at a time sinking slowly into our hearts. After we chew on the thought for a while it causes us to change our thinking on a subject or helps us to change our behavior in some aspect of our lives. Sometimes we observe these people of influence and perhaps desire to adopt an

41

attitude or demeanor they carry that is different from our own, so we model what we see in their lives.

One of these people of influence in my life is a banker friend of mine. His name is Alan Bragg. I would show up in his office and just talk to him and listen to his words, looking for pearls of wisdom that would help me to outline a path for my continued success. I wonder to this day if he thought for a second that anyone such as me (his youthful banking customer) would actually heed or even remember any of his words.

One day, in his office, I was again convincing him that I deserved another bank loan to buy another 18-wheeler and thereby produce more income and more business and also improve the overall success of his bank. As my manner was, I would throw out stupid comments that only could prove how green I was in business. In my closing argument to him I said *"After all, I have already run over a million dollars through your bank this year"*. All the banter and joking we were doing up to that point suddenly ceased. After a pregnant pause, my friend Alan said to me with all seriousness, *"Craig, you haven't kept a dime of it"*. The impact of what he said has followed me now and forever since that sobering moment. I had literally spent every penny that hit my bank account. Oh yeah, I knew how to grow a company from sweat equity, to take an idea from conception to infancy to fruition. But I had not learned how to keep any of my earnings.

Whenever I made more money, I would spend more money.

How often have you seen (or been) someone that would receive a pay raise and immediately (if not sooner) finance new furniture, a new car, or bigger home, thereby effectively spending all future gains? The problem really comes into fruition when the payments are due and the old pink slip comes in the pay envelope (you have just been laid off!).

You can bend without breaking

In bending your flagpole back, you won't break, I promise! The underlying moral here is to never spend all that you have. And if you find yourself needing extra income (and who doesn't?) check your outgo. See if there is something you can change that will *add* money back to the cash flow. Here are a few hints:

1. Do you realize that utilizing an ATM for cash withdrawals once a week could easily cost over $150.00 a year?
2. How about those late charges on your light bill 4 times in one year at $60.00 each?
3. Bounced check charges on a small bag of baby diapers, $36.00? (Yes, I've done it…)
4. Reconnect charges on your telephone, $100.00?
5. Finance charges on your credit card while making only

minimum payments, $unmentionable?

6. Checking account charges vs. a free checking or even an interest-bearing account $160.00?

7. Interest on a gas card vs. paying cash $323.00? (You'll still spend the same amount on fuel with or without the card but there are no finance charges for cash purchases!)

8. Fru-fru coffee drink daily @ $4 X 300 days. (What?? $1,200??)

9. Did you know that your insurance premium is cheaper when you pay the whole premium up front vs. financed by the insurance company for monthly installments? (Another $116.00 saved annually.)

Get the picture yet? Add all these together; add some of your own items to the list.

Now answer me this: *Is the key to your income the outgo?*

7 ♦ Put Your Mouth Where the Money Is!

The seventh rule of holes:

Never spend on a promise

Spending on a promise

Don't spend your money before you have it. If you have the promise of big bucks on the horizon, take it from my experience (and the experience of countless others), don't spend it before you have it.

A deal is not a deal until the money is in the bank!

The promise of future insurance settlements is not a reason to change your zip code either. A death in the family and a promised inheritance does not justify rushing out to buy a new automobile. A new job promotion that comes with a pay raise is not the go-ahead to buy a bass boat. The wise thing to do is to wait for the CIF (cash in fist)—that is, money on the old barrelhead.

Case in point: A good friend of mine was selling a pizza store that he had owned outright for years. The contract was signed and the deal went to the bank with a big "thumbs up" from the

45

lender. Consequently, while the deal was at the bank and waiting for a final business appraisal, my friend started building a new restaurant in a nearby town. His new store was really looking great; he found a super deal on restaurant equipment; everything was peaches and cream. Problem was, he didn't have the money to complete the new store until the sale of the old store actually funded.

Anyone care to hazard a guess as to what happened next? Well, fortunately for my friend, the store he sold actually ended up funding...six months later than expected. In the meantime, my friend had to borrow big money for completing the new store. A building remodel that should have been complete in 4 weeks was held up time after time because of lack of cash. My friend paid for at least 3 extra months of rent on the building just getting it ready to sell food. The interim loans cost him unnecessary interest payments on loans that he never could have afforded if the original pizza store sale had somehow failed. *And* he almost suffered the embarrassment of having started something he couldn't finish.

But an even greater faux-pas was that this friend of mine also had placed the successful business that he owned outright at risk of financial ruin if the sale had failed.

A deal is not a deal until the money crosses the palm!

46

I've known a few people who have been involved in lawsuits resulting in promised tax-free settlements. One family I know ran out and bought (owner financed actually) a $1.5 million-dollar home and extremely shiny and costly SUV after a jury tentatively awarded them a $4 million+ settlement. They even went on an expensive family resort vacation to Disney for 2 whole weeks. Problem was there were pesky little award limit laws in that state—along with the hefty cut promised to the various lawyers, medical bills to settle, and some very surprising incidental costs tagged to the whole mess.

As it turned out, this nice family, who was wrongly harmed by another's negligence, *after 16 more months of settlement arbitration*, received a cash balance of just under $400,000. Care to guess what happened next? Away goes the shiny SUV. The expensive home was forfeited and sold at a net loss of just over $120,000-uh, cash. These nice people were consequently both shocked and devastated. They already had spent almost half of the final settlement on the promise of bigger money.

My friends in this case did manage to purchase a modest home outright and sock a little cash back into a quickly dwindling savings account. A couple of years later they mortgaged their cash home to pay bills and do extensive remodeling. I'd say that within 4 years they were back exactly where they started before the lawsuit—money spent on a promise. Another case of the rich getting richer and the poor...well, they'll always be around.

If you are pending a settlement, inheritance, or other windfall, my best advice is this: Wait! Let the chicks hatch. Get the check, deposit it a few days later and then wait some more. After the dust settles, dole out the funds carefully and wisely. Invest some. Treat yourself some. Give some of it away. You decide. It's your money—all of what's left. Don't blame the broken system either. It's just broken. Be realistic about promised money.

Also, remember this catchy little anecdote as you navigate life:

A fool and his money soon party!

8 ♦ The Borrower is Servant to the Lender

The eighth rule of holes:

Never a borrower be

Borrowing money can be a real pitfall. Leveraging money and assets can be a tremendous tool to be used only with great caution and trepidation. Borrowing money because we have some kind of *entrepreneurial seizure* is sheer folly. *Leveraging* money and assets to make more money is in my opinion one of the few legitimate reasons to borrow money.

When you borrow on tomorrow, you often have to borrow again tomorrow

against the next day

because you already spent tomorrow's earnings today.

Does this make sense? Read it again a little slower…

When you borrow on tomorrow, you often have to borrow again tomorrow

against the next day

because you already spent tomorrow's earnings today.

Now, go back and reread it out-loud to yourself and then think about it some more before you read on.

Easy credit

The system of easy credit for perceived essentials has created a system that enslaves the borrower to future payments, but even worse than that, it captures the borrower's assets—both today's and tomorrow's—and can prevent the borrower from investing in things that would produce income for both today and tomorrow.

Instead of an investment made today, the money for a down-payment is gone for a great looking car or play-pretty today (that will also look a little older tomorrow). Unfortunately, tomorrow you are still paying for the car or gizmo-gadget while the new models are coming out with even *more* value to offer than ever before! And while you are looking at your now used and outdated car or product, the TV announcer incredibly states, *"There has never been a better time to buy a new model than right now!"*

"But I haven't paid for the first one", you lament—just before the announcer (as if he has read your mind) says, *"And we are offering more for your trade-in now than ever before in history"*! So, your logic says, "But I owe more than the shiny object is worth…" and again the mind-reading commercial airing salesman counters your objection: *"Are you trapped and upside down on your gizmo? Not to worry. We will accept almost any terms to get you into our shiny new one!"*

Your good sense still presides and you tell yourself to think about it for a few days. Again, the telepathic envoy pipes in: *"Hurry in today because this offer is over at midnight tonight!"*

Do you see where I am going with this? Smells like a big fat hole to me. Remember rule number 1? If the hole is getting deeper, you have to stop digging. No more borrowing on tomorrow's paycheck. Stop incurring any new debt. Warning Will Robinson! Red alert! Damage control! Once you stop digging the deeper hole, you can start devising a way out of your hole.

Where does the dirt from your hole go?

As a child I remember digging holes in an empty lot in the neighborhood. Other children got involved and our collective goal was, of course, to dig a hole to China. The deeper we got, the wider the hole became and one thing I noticed was that the dirt we were excavating was piling up higher and higher. Because of a lack of foresight, we actually ended up halting the digging to move our pile of dirt away from our growing canyon, as the dirt was beginning to fall back into the hole seemingly as much as we were removing it. Soon we had mountains of dirt surrounding us.

Finally, a concerned parent of one of the neighborhood children stopped our project by deeming the work dangerous to anyone or thing that might fall into the hole at night. The main take-away I learned from this childhood experience was this:

When you are digging a hole, the dirt has to go somewhere!

Other people build financial mountains out of your little molehills

If you are digging a financial hole, the dirt from your hole is helping to build a mountain somewhere else. Somewhere else and *someone else's* mountain, that is. Other people use the dirt from the hole that you are digging to build their empirical mountain of cash. If you are currently digging a hole, but would rather be building a mountain, think about where your dirt is going.

If the hole you are digging is a proverbial money pit, a cash rut, a hole in the earth surrounded by dirt into which you throw money, then the pay dirt that you are throwing out of your hole is being picked up by someone else and used for the building of their cash mountain.

The "dirt" you are methodically tossing out of your financial hole as you dig is actually the interest you pay on loans, the late penalties if and when they occur, the depreciation losses on new shiny objects, and many other misc. transfer fees, commissions, and carrying charges incurred. Some of this pay dirt is lost when you spend more than you can afford, and especially when you pay too much for something. These many fees and charges shift money from your "hip national bank" into someone else's "mattress national bank".

Probably the main difference between a cash mountain and a

money pit is a little time and some money savvy. When I say time, I'm talking about the weeks, months, and years it often takes for investments to mature. When I say money savvy, I'm not talking about bookkeeping 101, I'm talking about seeking good return on investments, making wise consumer choices, and avoiding the financial holes and money pits.

When you see someone else digging a hole, (throwing away money), think about how someone else is cashing in on their dough gaffe (clumsy money mistake). Now take this thought one step further: what if you were the one making the 18% interest compounded daily? Then start thinking about how you can invest to capture portions of this free-flowing river of cash. This kind of thinking often takes a paradigm shift—moving past the boundaries and thinking outside of the box. Repent of your former ways. Move the parameters of your finances by shifting your modus operandi (M O—method of operation). Start by doing things the opposite of losing money by gathering pay dirt from where other people are tossing it.

9 ♦ Never a Lender Be?

The ninth rule of holes:

Never loan money to friends and family

Lend money and you'll smart for it

Now let's deal with the lender part. I'm talking about lending money to a friend, a relative, a co-worker and I am not talking about investment lending (which can be both risky and lucrative).

About loaning to friends and family:

Never, never, ever, ever, loan money to a friend or relative!

I once owned some thriving businesses that employed over 50 employees. There never failed to be a week in which at least one employee would approach me with a personal financial emergency such as overdue rent, or a disconnect notice for their electricity service, or mama's urgent dental needs—you name it... Being the benevolent person that I am, I would loan them the money to see them past their immediate challenge by sending them to a secretary for a check made out to the utility company, landlord, dentist, or whoever. The employee would make arrangements with the bookkeeper to repay the debt by a weekly deduction from their already limited paycheck. As a result of this

54

practice, I ultimately lost many of these employees within a few weeks of the loan *and usually lost the whole loan amount also!*

This both puzzled and hurt me to see valued employees consistently disappear soon after a loan. I was actually becoming quite disconcerted and quickly drew the conclusion that lending money to an employee almost always ended in disappointment. My bafflement was never founded in the loss of the money but always in the loss of an employee. To top it off, I sometimes found out that the jobs some of these defecting employees went to actually paid less than they made with me.

I pondered this fact long and hard and looked at it from every perspective possible—including theirs. I finally concluded that if they were truly already behind in their finances and simply needed a few hundred bucks to "catch up" on the bills, but had to repay the money, they were actually *worse off* after a loan as they now took home less money per week after the weekly installment, but still had the same expenses hitting the budget from week to week. Often the only way out of this financial conundrum for them was to find another job outside of my company that did not deduct the weekly payment or that allowed them more working hours for more weekly wages in their paycheck.

I came to the wonderful conclusion that employee loans were very bad (I'll explain the words *wonderful conclusion* shortly). I saw that loaning money to a friend, family, or employee was almost

55

certainly fatal to that relationship. My problem was, that I was sad that I seemingly could not help the very people that I cared so much about without losing them.

It was at that point that I sought an answer to my dilemma outside of the "nine dots" of my own thinking. Then I realized that I still held the power to help the people that I loved and let them retain their dignity while maintaining a "no loans" policy to avoid hurting the relationships I had with them. The solution was so beautiful that I still remain in awe of this wonderful conclusion.

The philosophical rule I adopted to this dilemma was this: *If I could not afford to give them the money that they needed, I definitely could not and should not loan it to them.*

In other words:
If you cannot afford to give them the money, don't ever loan someone you care about money.

This is so simple and liberating. Just give it to them. After all, if you really want to help someone then don't set them further behind with debt payments; instead, give them a hand up. They are already behind; don't add to their misery. Simply give.

The most amazing thing happened when I applied this principle of "simply give". I retained my friends, employees, and relatives. No one got hurt. And even more amazing than that, I actually was being repaid by more people after simply giving than what I was being repaid as their loan officer. My employees certainly didn't need recurring debt loans if they were already in a financial hole. For once they were honestly being helped to get ahead of their finances. It was merely a side benefit that they almost always eventually repaid the cash *"gift"* out of love and respect rather than necessity or obligation.

So, in light of this I have to rewrite my prior statement of *"don't ever loan a friend or family money"* to this:

If you value your relationship with someone, don't ever loan them money.

If you want to really help them, give them the money!

Where less is more and more is less

Wise man says: *"the borrower is servant to the lender"*. So, which do you want to be? A servant that produces income for his master? Or a master that has servants building his mountain of wealth by digging for him? Wherever someone is ready to dig a hole, there is pay dirt and a willing worker to be found for building a financial mountain.

I now have a few questions for you: Which do you want to be—the boss or the peon? The master or the servant? The lender or the lendee? The one who pays money out or the one who takes money in? Is it better to pay money or to receive money? Better to dig a debt hole or build a mountain of wealth? The difference between borrower and lender is often simply a matter of perspective, decision, and solid commitment mixed with the tenacity to follow through. After you make the decision bolstered with commitment to build a mountain vs. digging a hole, it is now a matter of "less is better than more" when it comes to paying interest on loans or buying luxuries, and "more is better than less" in the realm of investing your money and reaping benefits.

10 ♦ Cause and Effect of Giving

The tenth rule of holes is:

What goes around comes around!

While smiles foster smiles, frowns often cause others to flee if they don't want to frown with you. Taking this idea a little further, generosity begets generosity and good will toward humankind, but miserly behavior generates misery, hardships, and curses. I believe that before humankind appeared on the face of the earth, the universal law of cause and effect was written and imposed upon the universe as we know it to be.

The word karma perhaps sums up the universal law of cause and effect. We've all heard these adages: "Karma's gonna get you baby!" or "What goes around comes around." or "you reap what you sow". These sayings are reflecting the basic understanding of how principles of *What goes around comes around* work in the world. The word karma is partially and broadly defined by Merriam-Webster as "...a force considered as affecting the events of one's life..." Karma can be oversimplified by dividing it into two simple categories: good or bad. If you consider our word karma to be the fruit of sowing and reaping, the fruits are either sweet or sour, depending on the nature of the seeds sown (actions performed).

Literally, everything we say and do affects what's going to happen to us in the future. This is because of the universal law of cause and effect that works indiscriminately for all; yet, there is no exact formula that guarantees how these karmic reactions manifest—but they do manifest both inwardly and outwardly. I would go so far as to say that internalized karma affects our mental and our physical health. Externally manifested karma produces results for all to see. Let's suffice it to say that everything you do either has a benefit or it has a consequence— some easy to see by all and some hidden (for now) from all.

In simpler terms: If you bang your head on the wall you get a headache. If you get a good night's sleep you function better. If you borrow money today you pay both the principle and the interest later. If you save up and pay cash, you own your things outright—no interest due. If you are late on your mortgage payment, too often you could lose your home. If you pay on time every time your credit score goes up and up.

In an essay written by Madhu Pandit Dasa in November of 2011, he offers one of three logical conclusions he considered when facing bad karma[8]:

---

[8] Dasa, Pandit. "Karma: What Goes Around Comes Around?" *The Huffington Post*, TheHuffingtonPost.com, 11 Jan. 2012, www.huffingtonpost.com/gadadhara-

1. God is cruel for letting things happen the way they are.

2. Things are happening completely by random chance and that there is no rhyme or reason behind them.

3. Perhaps in some inconceivable way, I had a hand in my own suffering, even if I wasn't able to recall what   I had done.

"I didn't like option two because I just couldn't accept that things were moving about randomly. I always felt there had to be some kind of order to the universe. Since I grew up believing in God, I was ready to wholeheartedly accept option one because this option allowed me to point a finger and express my anger and frustration at someone who I had worshiped all my life."

As for option three, Dasa eventually concluded *"…I couldn't really point a finger at anyone other than myself."*

Consider this: Emphysema is not necessarily a disease of what you breath in as much as it is a disease of taking in air and not giving it all back! The lungs get larger but breathing capacity gets smaller. The dead sea remains dead even though fresh water pours in daily through rivers and subterranean springs. The sea remains dead because it doesn't have an outlet! It can't give, it only takes.

Better to give than receive

Altruism is a state of selflessness where personal giving expects no return. Altruistic is the word used to describe when

pandit-dasa/karma-what-goes-around-comes-around_b_1081057.html. (Accessed online February 23, 2019).

you put other people's needs before your own, whether this involves holding a door open to allow someone else into the restaurant before you - giving up a prime parking space to someone when you arrived first - bringing cookies to a PTA meeting - to giving anonymous cash donations to good causes. Altruistic acts can include: Volunteering your time and service for a good cause, mentoring others within your area of expertise, performing random acts of kindness, returning lost items without receiving a reward, giving anonymously... Basically, altruism is simple and uncomplicated giving.

The altruism center of the brain is an actual, physical "deep brain structure" that kicks in when you observe a fellow human or even an animal in need[9]. The altruism center in the brain produces reflexive and instinctive prompts that ofttimes occur even before you can think. After all, we humans are social creatures and are hard-wired to help one another.

In reality is it really better to give than receive? YES! And this resounding yes is actually backed up by research. Neuroscience findings demonstrate that giving provides a powerful pathway for generating personal joy and improving overall health. What this means is that when you give selflessly and help others it is

---

[9] Ritvo, Eva. "The Neuroscience of Giving." *Psychology Today*, Sussex Publishers, 24 Apr. 2014, www.psychologytoday.com/us/blog/vitality/201404/the-neuroscience-giving. (Accessed online February 23, 2019).

beneficial for both your own mental health and your general wellbeing. This helps reduce stress, improves the emotional constitution, raises self-esteem, and these factors ultimately benefit your physical health.

1. Giving feels good

Giving generates a genuine warm fuzzy when you help others. It promotes positive physiological changes in the brain connected to happiness and the associated neurochemicals. Helping others can bring with it a euphoric rush from what I call the happiness trifecta of brain joy-juice. The neurochemical drivers of giving-generated happiness are dopamine, serotonin, and oxytocin[10]. Increasing any one if these brain juices will cause a boost in mood—and giving and helping actually stimulates all three! While euphoric rush events in the brain may be fairly short in duration, any post-rush brain activity is almost always followed by much longer periods of calm and serenity. (Interestingly, one study I read found that giving a certain amount of money to a preferred charity actually caused a bigger release of more dopamine than winning the same amount of money did.)

---

[10] Ritvo, Eva. "The Neuroscience of Giving." *Psychology Today*, Sussex Publishers, 24 Apr. 2014, www.psychologytoday.com/us/blog/vitality/201404/the-neuroscience-giving. (Accessed online February 23, 2019).

2. Giving brings a sense of belonging.

Ofttimes giving involves face-to-face engagement with others. This reduces tendencies for isolation and brings with it, feelings of belonging. Social activities such as giving as a volunteer worker reduce seclusion, loneliness, and depression. Helping others improves our own social support network, engages us in meaningful activity, encourages us to maintain a more physically active lifestyle, improves our self-esteem, and also distracts us from our own problems.

3. Giving brings perspective.

Viewing things from a new perspective can radically change your outlook on life. Giving to and helping others in need and perhaps less fortunate than yourself brings real-life perspective that will awaken you to realize how blessed you really are. A fresh viewpoint seen from another's predicament will often stop you from focusing on what you think you are missing out on. Reaching beyond your own idyllic desires while giving to those in need can even reduce self-imposed stress from perceived personal shortfalls. This will bring with it a more positive outlook on your own things and circumstances.

4. Giving is contagious!

Acts of kindness have the potential to make the world a happier place. Any act of kindness can improve self-confidence, self-control, internal happiness and optimism. Giving is also "paying it forward" which encourages others to repeat benevolent acts that they've experienced. Overall, giving in general promotes a more positive community.

5. Giving promotes good health.

Giving has been scientifically shown to reduce stress in the mind. Yet another 'side effect' of the stress reduction via giving is that reduced stress can boost your immune system and in turn help protect you against disease. This happens physiologically by way of reducing stress-induced, health-harming cortisol. When we—and that means both humans and animals—give care to another, we experience a drop in the stress hormone cortisol. In other words, when we do good things for others, we experience a reduction of stress in our own bodies.

Giving also reduces toxic emotions such as anger, hostility, and aggression—all of which have a negative impact on both your mind and body.

Giving altruistically can impact and increase how long you live. Studies show that older people who give care and support to others live longer than those who don't. And since giving reduces the negative impact of stress on health, reducing stress through altruistic acts can actually help us live longer and healthier lives.

Giving caveat:

I've always said: *"If you are going out to feed the poor, you'd better eat a big breakfast!"* In other words, don't overdo it. Juxtaposed to all the amazing benefits of altruistic giving is the harm of giving too much; that is, giving beyond your means and causing self-inflicted harm financially or physically. In the end, if you don't take care of your needs first—like eating a big breakfast before you rush off to help others—you yourself will become one of the needy you set out to help…and now someone else has to come feed you. Let's hope they ate a big breakfast first or we will all be in the proverbial soup.

Doing good makes good! ~ Paul Myer

11 ♦ Excuses Stink

The eleventh rule of holes:

Excuses are like rear ends!

Don't Make Excuses

Excuses are like rear ends! Everyone has one and some people show them off more than others. When you blame your shortcomings on other people or the fickle finger of fate and foul circumstances, you present yourself as a victim. When you accept responsibility for your own destiny outcome, you are then able to change your circumstances and rise above insurmountable challenges to become a victor. The main difference between a victim and a victor is that the perpetual victim gives up and succumbs to circumstances while offering only excuses—the valiant victor keeps on fighting until they overcome.

Did you know that Thomas Edison discovered at least 700 elements that did not make great light bulb filaments before he finally discovered one that did?

One of Thomas Edison's goals was to invent a suitable filament to produce a viable incandescent light. After Thomas Edison's seven-hundredth and some-odd unsuccessful attempts to invent an electric light bulb, he was asked by a *New York Times* reporter, "How does it feel to have failed seven hundred times?"

"…I have not failed 700 times. I have not failed once. I have succeeded in proving that those 700 ways will not work. When I have eliminated the ways that will not work, I will find the way that will work…." ~ Thomas Alva Edison[11]

The only way Thomas Edison could have possibly failed would have been if he had given up. If you fold in a card game you automatically lose by default *even if you had the winning hand!* And then…you have none to blame but yourself.

Winners never quit and quitters never win!

I had an economics professor teach his own hypothesis that it is a sociological fact that if you gathered all the money in the United States into one big pile, and then distributed it evenly to the entire population, within 3 years the same people would have all their money back again. This made-up scenario and hypothesis affirm the foregone conclusion in my mind that victims have been trained to remain victims and victors always persist until the victory is won.

I suppose that if you were the poor bloke in this scenario and the rich garnered their money back from you, your excuse could go something like: *"I guess that those people have a superior financial*

[11] *Quotefancy*, quotefancy.com/quote/916544/Thomas-A-Edison-I-have-not-failed-700-times-I-have-not-failed-once-I-have-succeeded-in. (Accessed online February 24, 2019).

savvy that I do not have." Or: *"Those people have always been lucky with money and stock markets and I have not."* And my favorite dumb excuse: *"He was born with a silver spoon in his mouth and I wasn't."* These words would resound with the obvious defeatist attitude displayed by a victim (aka loser) who doesn't want to be held responsible for their continuing circumstances.

Bottom line, excuses are worthless at the bank counter. Anyone can excuse all of the responsibilities away in denial but that still won't cash a check when the money just isn't there. And even if all the excuses were well-reasoned and legitimate, and none of the bad things were actually from some personal fault, this still cannot get anyone out of a hole. Excuses are permission to leave, check out, take a powder, duck away from circumstances and responsibility. Excuses only lead in a negative direction—ever.

Let's diverge on a rabbit trail and examine some real-world excuses for failure. But realize that humans actually only utilize about 3% of their actual brain capacity and resources. We can use this fact to help eliminate the heredity factor that we tend to excuse our shortcomings to.

1. "Little Johnny Jump-up can't read because he unfortunately got shorted a little in the brains department."

This is a lie from the pit of H. E. double hockey sticks. Little

Johnny can't read because he has not been presented with the right opportunity to learn as Little Johnny learns. If you do not agree with me on this point, then tell me how you can teach a 3-year old child with Down Syndrome to read when you present learning opportunities to them in short sessions at frequent intervals during the day for several months?[12] In this case it is only a matter of the right opportunities afforded to the child.

When little Johnny cannot read, society norms teach him to acquiesce. They make exceptions for his 'disability' and teach him how to cope with his situation with unending support and accommodations. All this is nice, warm, and fuzzy, but why settle for the disable label? I happen to know lots of parents fighting the odds and not accepting society's labels until both they and their child *are victorious*—not victims.

2. "Johnny Jump-up Senior is broke because it is his lot in life."

We often do the same thing to little Johnny Junior's dad financially in our society with social class labels and postures. When Johnny's dad cannot manage the budget on his factory wages, he goes broke, stays broke, and becomes labeled and

---

[12]Stellpflug, Craig. "Eye Development Milestones." *Child Eye Developmental Milestones*, www.realhealthtalk.com/Eye_Developmental_Milestones.html. (Accessed online February 23, 2019).

limited. He easily falls into debt holes in the which he is taught by societal norms to conform and succumb to—along with possibly acquiescing to the lifelong fate of skull drudgery and common labor. Johnny Senior is offered bankruptcy as a temporary solution and they give him counseling and maybe even drugs to help him cope. And here comes the dangling carrot: After all, if we don't offer Johnny Senior a little relief and respite once in a while, he may actually give up completely and become a permanent burden on society. Another rat lost off the treadmill...

Let's say that even if Johnny Senior can successfully manage the budget and avoid a few debt holes, is this all he wants out of life? To be a faithful factory worker all his born days? To raise a quiet little family in a quiet little town and teach his children how to be quiet little factory workers just like their dad? Where is the human potential in that? To retire in front of a big screen TV after 25 years hard labor at the gristmill and then convalesce the rest of his life watching his favorite movies all day long while receiving the occasional visits from his grandchildren? Folks, I've seen this happen! I guess that this isn't really that bad of a situation if Johnny Senior is content and satisfied with his life. At least in his contentment he won't be making excuses.

3. "The glass ceiling has Janie Jump-up limited and trained like a flea. She thinks she can only go as far as the ceiling will allow."

Speaking of human potential, innate to every human being is the ability and desire to better their life. Inside every individual is an inborn ability to excel beyond one's peers and teachers, an innate desire to invent and achieve and find challenges to overcome, an inherent quality that will seek to heal the sick and comfort the afflicted. Inside the basic human character is also a built-in desire to be accepted by our peers and to become and remain productive and wise.

If anything less than these attributes is evident in a man or woman's life, it is caused by either learned behaviors or a blatant lack of opportunities to develop these characteristics.

Examine your own words and attitudes. Did what I just say above really tick you off, or did it set you to thinking? A thinking person will often compare their own thinking with the thinking of others. They will evaluate and compare other people's words, actions and attitudes to their own. They will accept or reject other's input in whole or in part. They may even toss out a few of their old habits and ideas in light of new ones that they deem worthy of personal approval.

A person of limited capacity for change will quickly condemn and throw away anything that contradicts his own egocentric ways and teachings; thereby effectively limiting his own human potential.

So, what's your excuse? Are you or are you not solely responsible for your own choices and destiny? Discovering and developing opportunities is what it takes to change any of your own situations. If finances are your biggest challenge then educate yourself about money. If your vocabulary is limited then read the dictionary. If you are dyslexic then patch one eye for a few weeks and see if it helps. If your memory is short then take a memory course. If you need a degree to advance in your career then go get one!

Learn how to succeed and then pass the legacy on to your children. Show them and teach them how to expand their opportunities by letting them see your own efforts, successes, and even temporary failures. Teach them how to obey the laws of the land but not be limited by false rules and mandates imposed by glass ceilings, social classes, and temporary circumstances.

Rise up and take responsibility!

Always take responsibility for your own predicaments and actions. Also, know the difference between laws and social class rules. Laws are made and enforced to protect both ourselves and others from wrongs and harms. Laws of man are not made to be broken but rather to be amended as necessary. Laws of man are there to keep civil order and protect lives and property. Social class rules and norms are there to be challenged, stretched, and changed. Social class rules are imposed to keep the "undesirables" out of a certain social class, clique, or club while keeping the desirable ones in—but social class rules are not laws! Glass ceilings are imposed to protect the lofty ones but glass ceilings are not laws, and can be broken with impunity. Likewise, educational limits may prevent you from attaining a certain job, but they are merely hurdles to be overcome and not laws.

Bottom line: If you mess up; own it. If you fall short; stretch it next time. If it is a social rule or norm; challenge it. If it is a law; respect it.

The reason that we have so many laws in our great land and so many lawyers to argue them is that people in general will not take responsibility for their own actions!

12 ♦ The Chicken Coop Effect

The twelfth rule of holes is:

It's hard to soar with eagles when you hang with chickens!

The parable of the eagle who thought he was a chicken

There once was a farmer who found an eagle's nest in a fallen tree after a storm. One of three eggs made it through the devastation and was still intact in the topsy-turvy treetop. On a whim, the farmer took the one intact egg home and put it into the nest of one of his brooding hens. The egg hatched along with 10 or so chicken eggs in the nest and the surrogate mother hen took the eagle chick for one of her own. As the eagle chick grew it learned how to scratch the ground and peck for grain along with the other chickens. The eagle even learned how to hop and briefly fly for a few feet just as all the other chickens in the hen yard did. The eagle never realized he was any different from the other fowl that it grew up with. The eagle had never even dreamed or thought of soaring to great heights and roaming the skies.

This eagle was limited by the opportunities afforded him.

The farmer eventually began to fear for the lives of his chickens, thinking that the eagle would learn to eat chickens just

75

like the eagles that were born among their own kind. So, he took the eagle to a remote place and turned it loose. The poor, misplaced eagle was now lost and all alone. When the local crows discovered that this particular eagle would not fly and eat their young, they began to harass him diving at him and pecking him viciously trying to avenge the loss of their own chicks to other eagles that ate them.

Driven by desperation to escape the incessant onslaught by the crows, the eagle tried running and hopping like a chicken would, flying for a few feet and then landing unceremoniously in a heap with a crow or two pulling out feathers and slicing at him with their claws. One time he hopped and flew so far that he actually outdistanced his tormentors briefly. In short order, the now bedraggled and hurting eagle figured out that he could actually fly. Necessity drove him to figure out that he could fly farther and higher and faster than his tormentors.

Necessity is the often the mother of invention.

Soon the young eagle was flying the heights and resting on the mountaintops where he belonged. No longer limited by his opportunities, he soon learned how to behave like other eagles.

Are you an eagle that is cleverly disguised as a chicken? Are you so completely attired, that not only do you fool everyone around you, but you fool yourself also? Unlike the eagle, you and

I can make and choose our own opportunities.

But the story is not always quite as clear and easy as this one. When we force ourselves out of the chicken yard (or get tossed out as it may be), and start to associate with a different realm of people, we will soon encounter the crows—that is, *the dream-stealers* and *naysayers, mockingbirds,* and other nasty vermin—just like the crows that pecked at the unwitting eagle.

When we encounter the crows in our life we will:

A: Succumb to the adversity and retreat to the bogus safety of the chicken yard.

B: Rise above the challenges and learn to soar with other eagles and rule the skies.

C: Compromise with the crows and learn to live somewhere in the middle, always short of the glory and grandeur available to us.

My main point here is that we can make our own opportunities and change our own circumstances. Do not settle to be an eagle disguised as a chicken!

Cases and points: It's hard to go beyond where you have been led and taught

I personally believe that every child born into this world is a potential genius. I also know that every child born into this world is limited by the opportunities afforded them. For instance: Rich people teach their young how to make and keep money (like the eagles' parents do), while poor parents teach their children how to survive on limited resources (like the chickens do). Mean parents tend to teach their young to be mean, math teachers somehow seem to gender little math whizzes, the car dealer teaches his child how to haggle, and so forth.

Not knowing what is available to you will limit you without you ever realizing it. I believe that we are all potential eagles and that some of us (who think and cluck like a chicken) will never rise above that mentality unless we first see and understand that it is available for us to soar with the eagles.

Training a flea

To train a flea you first place it in a glass jar. Then you stretch a piece of cellophane neatly over the opening. A flea can easily jump several feet; however, when this one tries to jump out of the jar, it now bumps its head every time. Within minutes the flea is completely trained not to jump high enough to bump its head. You can now remove the cellophane and rest assured that the newly trained flea will never try to escape by jumping higher than the opening of the jar.

In business this is called a "glass ceiling". You can see the lofty positions in the sky but keep bumping your head on the limits imposed by the ones who rule the lofty realms.

Some of us have been trained like a flea to only jump so high.

Training an elephant

To train an elephant you first stake him to a large stump using a heavy chain. The elephant will pull and strain for a while until he finally gives up and no longer pulls at the restraint. You can now remove the chain and tie him back up with a flimsy rope on a wooden stake and he will not attempt to pull away.

Some of us have been trained like the elephant to not resist constraints.

Training a fish

To train a fish not to eat other fish you place it in a tank with a glass divider in it. On one side lives the fish that is in training and on the other side of the clear partition you put some tasty minnows. The fish will lunge at the minnows and bump into the unseen boundary until he figures out that it just cannot eat these delicate little treats. At this point you can remove the divider and let the minnows swim all around the predator fish. Even if you forget to feed the fish and this guy becomes very hungry, it does not eat the minnows because it is convinced that it will only bump its nose trying.

Some of us cannot see opportunity even if it bumps us in the nose.

Training a herd of pigs

To train a herd of pigs, you install an electric fence around the perimeter of their boundaries. After a few days you can turn off the electric shocker and eventually take it completely down, the pigs will never go beyond the perimeter set by the original electric fence.

Sometimes we live and die in the perimeter others confine us to—and that we confine ourselves to.

Training horses

To train a horse to stay off of a fence you put up a strand of electric wire on the fence you wish to protect. You then tie little pieces of rags to the electric fence wire. After being introduced to the shock of the electricity when the horse ventures upon the fence, the horse will forever associate the rags on the wire to the shock. Any old piece of wire, or even string, with a few little rag pieces tied on it will now keep the horse away from the fence.

We are often "once bitten, twice shy" and never challenge our existing premises.

Retraining humans

If you just happen to be a human reading this book (and you are not a flea, fish, horse, pig, or elephant), you have the innate and God-given abilities to dream along with the actual potential to reach that dream. With this endowment you can cleverly invent means out of any situation—Uh, once you are made aware of the problem. Your super-human abilities always allow you to analyze and plan remedies. Your cortical brain and critical thinking capacity allow you to re-educate past a learned behavior and pretended limitation unlike the flea, fish, horse, pig, and elephant.

Always challenge any and all limitations placed upon you. Just never, ever hurt or take advantage of anyone else in the process!

13 ♦ Declaration of Belief Yields Receipt of Confession

The thirteenth rule of holes:

You become what you say you are

It should be safe to say that what everyone reading this book is looking for is success. Success breeds success and we all possess an inborn desire to succeed. Something to consider about successful people is that they will seldom, if ever, entertain the possibility of failure. They almost never talk about the possibility of failure and they absolutely believe that they are successful. They literally become what they believe and talk about. In short, they talk and walk success.

If you truly desire success, then why would you entertain the words of the dream-stealers that tell you that you cannot succeed? When someone tells you that you cannot succeed, take a quick glance at his or her lives. Are they living their dreams? Are they successful? Do they want you to be a success? Or are they jealous that you might "catch a break" and leave them behind? After all, misery does love company. If success breeds success, then it naturally follows that failure would also breed failure. If you lay with dogs, you soon come up with fleas. You either soar with the eagles or flop with the chickens!

So, let me ask you this: If you wanted to become a successful farmer, whom would you go to for mentoring and instruction? A dirt-poor old farmer who has been in the farming business for years but never really made a successful living? Or would you go to the biggest and most prosperous farmer you could find and then model what they did to be successful? Of course, you would want to be studying at the feet of the winner, right? You would listen to the winner's words and begin to model the winner's speech and habits. If you learn anything from the poor farmer it should be *what not to do.*

Likewise, if you hang out with dream-stealers and people that use the words **can't do**, you will absolutely become one yourself. I call these fowl friends the mockingbirds. Keep them near to you and you will learn their ways whether you want to or not. If you hang out with winners, the same thing will happen; you will learn their ways and words and become a winner yourself.

---

[13] Ingraham, Christopher. "The Richest 1 Percent Now Owns More of the Country's Wealth than at Any Time in the Past 50 Years." *The Washington Post*, WP Company, 6 Dec. 2017, www.washingtonpost.com/news/wonk/wp/2017/12/06/the-richest-1-percent-now-owns-more-of-the-countrys-wealth-than-at-any-time-in-the-past-50-years/?noredirect=on&utm_term=.630658f0d5ce. (Accessed online February 23, 2019).

Let's take a moment to consider some bare facts about success: 99% of people will live their lives in a pattern of mediocrity. Only a mere 1% of people will become wealthy in their lifetime as a result of their own efforts[13]. This leaves a very narrow margin of successful people to hang out with. The *only* difference between the 99% and the 1% is their confessed beliefs pure and simple. No one talked the 1% out of his or her dreams and potential. Instead, the 1% took charge of life and the 1% did not settle for mediocrity. The 1% did not accept the J O B (an acronym for **J**ust **O**ver **B**roke) as their potential in life. The 1% followed and learned from other successful people and made their own opportunities. The 1% also learned to confess the positives and reject the negatives.

Another sobering fact is that less than 5% of people will ever achieve financial independence in their entire lifetime. Bottom line, all excuses aside, everyone will ultimately choose and confess their own socio-economic path in life. You will however, always have a lot of volunteer help choosing which path you stay on. Of course, friends, family, co-workers, neighbors, and pedestrians will offer their say in an attempt for influence in financial matters—make no mistake about that! Everyone loves to interject their opinion for free. Their opinions and words will always have an effect on you if you allow it. It is your duty to choose to accept or reject failure, accept or reject success, or live somewhere in the broad and obscure plain that lies between the two.

You can let the words of the mockingbirds drive you to mental and financial bankruptcy or you can use their negative words as a springboard that drives you to succeed. *If someone's words do not promote your dream, you are free to throw them away!*

To succeed you absolutely must get serious about your words. You absolutely have to take verbal action and maintain course. You must not fail. It takes self-discipline, self-control, self-mastery, and constant action to maintain a positive confession.

Control over your thoughts and words will, without a doubt, be your hardest challenge on the road to success. I am issuing a challenge to everyone reading this book today. For the next 24 hours, you cannot think about failure, only success. And you can only talk about your dream for success, your goals and desires and nothing else for the next whole day. Visualize what to do with the prosperity and be comfortable with success. It absolutely won't be easy; however, if for these 24 hours you can strive for this oral victory, you will begin to reshape the future. If you continue this challenge for a few more days, it will begin to form a subconscious habit of successful thinking that will change your life forever.

For the next 24 hours, repeat your goals and dreams to yourself and confess them to others. Dream about your success and how it will change your life. Place pictures of what you desire in front of your eyes. Keep your thoughts consistent with this visualized success and toss aside all other thoughts as they encroach upon your mind. And don't get discouraged because the old thoughts keep coming up—just change your mind immediately. Remember, it's never wrong to have a negative thought. It is however, counterproductive to success to entertain a negative thought and let it fester and breed in your mind.

This is what I say about the inevitable dream-stealers: Identify them and distance yourself from their voices. Or better yet, if possible, have them join your quest and help you to avoid negatives by not voicing them around you; but rather, have them remind you of your dreams and goals. Success breeds success and maybe, just maybe, they too will join you in success.

And finally, stay faithful to the program. Consistency is the only thing that brings consistent results. Consistently surround yourself with successful people, thoughts, and programs. You will become a winner and stay a winner.

14 ♦ Work Honestly and Work Hard

The fourteenth rule of holes:

All work is honorable

All work is honorable according to Voltaire (a classic writer from years ago). In his book titled Candide he writes: *"…work keeps away three evils: boredom, vice, and need."*

So, I now say once again: All work is honorable.

In my repertoire of business ventures, I bought and sold a few restaurants. I had several at once and didn't have time to manage them so I hired a manager for overseeing all of them. On occasion I would pop in to one of these restaurants and pitch in at whatever was needed. I scrubbed a few toilets or washed some dishes, swept floors, cooked and generally covered whatever post needed the most help. One evening I was a waiter because that station was apparently suffering. Three waitresses were working, disgruntled completely and obviously not keeping up. Customers were suffering. So, I bussed tables, took orders, delivered food and served complimentary coffee as an aperitif.

Within 20 minutes everything was caught up and one of the waitresses decided to bug out in the middle of supper rush—leaving me to fill the vacancy for her shift. However, my enthusiasm had already caught on to the remaining waitstaff and remarkably, even though we got even busier yet, every table was served well and no one was missed. The funniest part was that the customers didn't know I was the owner. Two of the waitresses didn't know either at first. When the supper rush finally slowed, the remaining waitresses gawked at the amount of the tips I had taken in. I had out-performed them all! But you see, I wasn't working for tips. I was working to serve the guests with everything I had in me. I worked honorably and whole-heartedly. Not because I was the owner, but because that is how I set my heart.

Don't Fight Over a Pig Wallow!

Another food service observation I made was that people fight over the darndest things! At one time I actually had people cutting each other's throats for an assistant shift manager's position. Remembering that all work is honorable, watch out when pride and ego rule, because emotions and knee jerks will certainly abound. The big question: Is the position worth the dirty fight and cattiness? Lie and cheat and spread gossip to discredit someone else to make his or her own self look like a better choice for the position? To be Lord of the flies? Are you all hett up over ruling a pig wallow? Never a pretty sight to see. And did you really want what you've gotten after you get it? Most importantly, are you willing to sacrifice personal integrity for temporary gain? If so, you don't deserve to be my assistant shift manager with a dollar an hour pay raise.

Work with your heart and not your ego

I have another saying to go along with *"All work is honorable"* and that is *"All work is also important"*. I can illustrate my point this way: Which is more important, the preacher at the pulpit or the person cleaning the toilets? I guarantee one thing, if the person cleaning the toilets fails, the congregation might have a bigger challenge listening to the preacher over the smells than otherwise! If the toilets at one of my establishments reeked, no matter how wonderful the cuisine… well, you get the point. As the restaurant owner I was never above cleaning the bathrooms or busting suds in the dish sink.

Go ahead, say it: *"But you're the owner! You're invested in the business."* My response to you is this: *"I cleaned toilets with the same heart of service long before I became an owner."*

Yes, I have yet another anecdotal story or two for this heart principle. Bear with me and I'll tell it to you. I was going to college and working nights part-time at a badly run convenience store. I was hired on a moment's notice and not even trained for the job. A few nights later the store was in bad shape and growing worse. The manager jumped me about cleaning the store at night and I said *"Wha...? This is your fault for not training me."* Well, she was livid and read the riot act to me and proceeded to work ALL NIGHT beside me in a possessed fury of cleaning, sweeping, mopping, stocking, and scrubbing. At 6 a.m. she sent me out the door at the end of my shift and told me rather bluntly, and colorfully, that I had to do everything on this mad-woman cleaning list every night from now on or I was fired. I retorted, *"Oh, you expect me to do the work of two people in one night AND wait on customers?"*

I almost quit on the spot but miraculously held my tongue against the severe cursing and threats coming from this manager. Later that day I met with a mentor of mine and voiced all the complaints I had held back from releasing on her. I told my mentor that I was going to call the head office and surely get her fired. The mentor listened patiently and sagely showed me how I had poked the proverbial bear. He told me I was going to lose my job because I was disrespectful. He told me that either I whipped this situation by doing my job or the situation would whip me

90

again and again until I got over myself. Hard words for young ears and I almost told my mentor to stick his advice elsewhere.

Again, I held my tongue by some miracle and mulled the advice over for a couple of days instead. The next time I clocked in to my shift I grabbed some gusto and declared that the manager wasn't going to win—I was! I cleaned and I swept and mopped and stocked and scrubbed most of the night. Suddenly it was 5 a.m. and I was done. The store sparkled just as it had the other night with two of us working—and I still had an hour left. When the manager showed up at 6, fully expecting to fire me, I apologized to her and told her I would do everything on that list every time I worked. She smiled and thanked me and allowed me to stay working for her.

A few weeks later a frequent customer offered a job to me that paid almost triple. He said he needed conscientious workers like me. Of course, I accepted!

This story also leads us to yet another gem of truth which is a tried and true statement: *"It is easier to find a job when you have a job."* But remember that the principle truth in this chapter is to work and to work heartily no matter what the job is that you have committed to do because *all work is honorable.*

15 ♦ The Explosion Contemplation

The fifteenth rule of holes:

Understand your own limits

How much pressure can you handle?

People always let you know when they have had all they can handle. They don't always voice it but there are signs and signals to see. Sometimes we fail to see the signs and get caught in the percussion of someone else's blowout. This happens when a pressure situation becomes more than they can bear. You know, the straw that breaks the camel's back.

Most people however, continue and push and go until they fall out completely. They usually collapse in a negative, implosive manner that just simply takes them out. Sometimes, however, in the extreme, someone will do the opposite and explode outward. They may even destroy the whole project they are involved in (pulling the whole building down on top of themselves and everyone around them, destroying everything).

Some people are wise enough to call their limit before they

break. They may gracefully bow out of the pressure situation they are in and retreat to a position they can handle. This is a rare quality sometimes deemed "a copout" by the bystanders. Some people seem to be impervious to pressure situations and barrel on through the most ridiculous situations. Bystanders often call these people "feckless and irresponsible". But who cares what the bystanders think?

Why the contrast? Some people are so tough in pressure situations that if you had to eat them, they would be way too tough to chew. These people can lead a patrol through enemy lines standing up and never duck a single bullet. They could go through a paint ball war getting hit in the mask and never flinch an eye. They could stand between two passing freight trains hurtling by each other and nonchalantly hum a tune the whole time. Other people fold at the first sign of adversity. So, who is right and who is wrong here? Probably neither, so don't judge how someone else handles pressure. I say this because we often compare and judge what we see going on with the external appearances in someone's life—good or bad—with our own inner thoughts and experiences—good or bad.

In your own life, when the pressure mounts, when the temptation to fold and retreat looms before you, consider this: *Is this your true limit?* Do you want to "cap things off" and make this the boundary? After all, there is absolutely no shame in finding your true limit and remaining within it. Shame in this case only comes with the regret of an early retreat.

When it comes to pressure I say: *"Show me how much pressure you can handle and I'll show you how far you can go in business."*

The lesson of the woods

While I was growing up, my family lived in rural Minnesota for a while. We rented an old farmhouse at the end of a long and narrow dirt lane. On one side of the lane was cornfields and on the other was a well-established grove of trees. Problem was, in the winter, after making a trail with the snowblower, we could be headed up the lane only to meet a farmer coming down the lane. This meant that someone had to reverse their rear-wheel drive vehicle all the way back to the slippery end to allow the other to pass. My dad got the great idea the next spring to widen the lane by taking out a row of the outlying trees and gravelling the road to make it two-lane.

What happened next was a life's lesson for me. That summer a windstorm came through and toppled a number of trees in the center of the grove. This grove had withstood many years of windstorms and tornados but couldn't manage to stand up after the outward-facing trees were removed. You see, the winds and storms had challenged the outer trees for decades, causing their roots to go deep and wide while protecting the inner woods from the blustering winds. The inner trees lacked the depth to withstand the challenge.

Are you an inner grove tree or an outer grove tree? It takes both to make a grove.

To another point: The reason plants have trouble growing in a space station is there is no gravity to challenge the plant and no wind to buffet the plant and grow the fibers that strengthen it.

When it comes to life I have always said: *"The harder the soil, the hardier the plant."*

Here is a poem I wrote some decades ago:

Lesson of the water

When you have burdens in your heart that many troubles bring
Remember, it is the rocks in the brook that make it sing
For the water takes these hurdles and turns them into song
And if you listen to its wisdom you'll learn to sing along

Consider the stream, if a wall is there to stem its flow
It gathers its strength until over the top it will go
Because the bigger the barrier the stronger it builds
Therefore an even greater triumph the victory yields

You see if a dam gets in its way the stream doesn't fret
Because worries are prepayment on a usury debt
So why pay a premium on a balance you don't owe
For fear is a negative result of what you don't know

All the water runs to the seas yet the seas are not filled
And its ultimate purpose our finite wisdom can't yield
So let us study the example that the water has shown
Then from uncertainties we won't ever borrow or loan

Regardless, wherever your strength lies, regardless of life's rocks in your stream, be happy. Rise to challenges. Push the limits if you wish. Push them harder, if that is within you.

16 ♦ How to Make Money Buying and Selling

The sixteenth rule of holes:

Buy low, sell high

Buying and selling for profit is an art. I was chatting with my banker friend (same one as earlier) and we were talking about a real estate purchase I had made. I actually managed to purchase it at a very good price at a time when the local markets were rebounding from a low. The market for houses was becoming strong and soon became a "seller's market". This means that the sellers can name their price a little above market price and sell at that higher price (as opposed to a buyer's market where the buyer names a lower price and wins because the market is weak). I just happened to buy this home at a reduced price and was going to sell at a very good mark-up. I made several thousand dollars on that deal because I was able to buy low and sell high.

As I continued the conversation with my banker the subject turned from real estate to cattle prices. Cattle at that time were at an all-time high in the local auction houses and a friend of mine had approached me to ask for a small personal loan for himself. He wanted to get into the cattle business because cattle prices were doing so well. I owned a few cows myself at the time and I mentioned the opportunity to my banker. My banker proceeded to tell about his experience, successes, and failures raising cattle. In the end my banker told me, "You don't buy cattle when the cattle prices are high. You buy cattle when the cattle prices are low and you sell them when the prices are high."

In other words, if you want to make money on purchased investments, you have to get a good deal on what you buy in the first place. The obvious best time to buy something is when the market is soft and the sellers cannot get their normal asking prices. The secret is that everything has a cycle that can be followed and often predicted. What goes up must come down is a rule of thumb—*most of the time.*

As a case in point: Watch what happens when people hear that the price of gold is going up. They buy gold waiting for it to go up higher. Lately sometimes it does, but more often it doesn't. In my opinion, this is the best time to be a seller of gold because the best time to sell something is obviously when the market is hot and the demand is up. Oh, and don't be afraid to let go of an investment before it peeks. If you can make a good return, even though the market may still rise a little (or may not), sell while the selling is good. So what if someone else makes a little more off of your sell? That's OK. You don't have to squeeze all of the juice out of the orange. If you try to get all you can get, the market could and often does turn like a bear and come crashing into a sell-off frenzy where everyone is hot to sell and get out from under a product. And that, my friend, is approaching the best time to buy.

What I am really saying here is this: When you shop for an investment, consider looking around at the things that people do not want. You can find a bargain with just a little time spent researching. You can also research and learn about the market cycles that have happened before with that product. Plot out the history and see how often the market for that product turns. Look for seasons, trends, triggers and other factors that come into play. Completely educate yourself, find others who invest in that product, learn the language of the market, find the buying and selling points, and don't be afraid to get your feet wet.

Supply and demand

Value is an amazing thing. If something is hard to find or even rare, the value of it goes up. Whole markets are driven by availability. If you want to sell copious amounts of a flu vaccination that may or may not even be effective, make it appear hard to get, short in supply, and expensive to buy. If you want to make health care insurance a precious commodity, go way up on the price, limit the services, and get really picky about who can have it. (In my opinion most health insurance plans offer very little value. Insurance companies glean a pretty premium to manage your money for health care. After all, they make money taking your money and paying your bill or they would be out of business in a hurry.)

You see, how something is presented affects the perceived value. Detailing a car before it is sold not only increases the shine-value of the car, but it increases the likelihood of a quicker sale. A better car that is not detailed out will bring a lesser price and also sell slower. The same piece of art stretched with fatter edges makes the art look much more impressive than if you stretched it on thin bars. Beer served in tall, thin glasses vs. short, fat glasses sells better because of the perception that you will get more beer in a tall glass. Green packaging colors for food and goods versus any other color gives the perception of health and sells more than a better product packaged with a different color.

Show an infomercial with good looking, trim people that have animated presence, and you will sell a heap more product than if you choose the wrong looking or dull person to showcase your product. Same product, different perception. Sharp dressed car salesmen sell more cars than the poorly dressed salesmen. Nothing different with the car quality—just the perception.

You only lose when you sell low

Yet another acquaintance of mine joined me for breakfast one day and lamented on and on about how much money he had just lost as a certain company stock plummeted in price. I could only ask him one question: *Why did you sell then?* His answer made me shake my head. *Oh, I didn't sell, I can't afford to actually lose that much money.* I knew then that he hadn't lost a single dime because he didn't actually sell. In fact, two years later the same stock rebounded and he sold most of it for a tidy profit. The moral of this story is that you only make or lose money as you buy and sell. That is why you buy low and sell high.

A little sage advice is to keep your higher risk ventures limited to what you can afford to lose if it flounders.

And remember the old adage "Nothing ventured, nothing gained."

Funding your high-risk investments

Here's another thinker for you. Do you personally have $2,000 in discretionary income set aside? (Discretionary income is money that you can spend on anything you need or want and do not have to rob Peter or Paul to come up with it.) Okay then, how about $600? $200? If you answered no to these money questions you probably feel very bad all of a sudden. If you feel bad all of a sudden, let it be a wakeup call. Especially if you have been out there working for years and just making ends meet.

What if the opportunity of the year came up and your neighbor was moving overseas and had to sell his collectable car, cheap? Discretionary cash could double or more for you in a case like that! What if you could buy some tax liens and receive a guaranteed 25% return in less than a year but you didn't have $1100 to buy in? How about a rare antique at a garage sale that is severely underpriced? Could you venture the cash without losing your electricity from nonpayment?

I have seen 50-year-old working adults lose out on deals because they didn't have a few hundred bucks of discretionary cash to invest in a venture after working hard for 32 years. Hoover syndrome (That sucks)! If this sounds like your life, look for the nearest exit from the sheep pen you are in and then don't go back! And always, always - buy low, sell high.

17 ♦ Thinking Outside the Box

The seventeenth rule of holes:

The Nine Dots Challenge

•   •   •

•   •   •

•   •   •

Pretend that these nine dots represent some personal challenge in life. Perhaps they represent your financial shortfall, educational limits, or even some physical disability. Now take these nine dots and a pencil. Using four straight lines, your challenge is to connect these nine dots while drawing only straight lines, consecutively and without lifting the pencil to start the next line. If you fail to solve your problem and connect all nine dots the first time, take a few more tries. If you still cannot solve this problem, don't give up! And don't read ahead until you have honestly tried and completely failed to connect these dots. Helpful hint: This can be done!

Remember that this challenge of connecting the nine dots represents a challenge in your life that you need to overcome. If you solved this problem easily, you either knew the answer already, are exceptionally visionary, or you are in the top 3% of scholared eggheads.

The wonderful solution to this challenge is to *think outside of the nine dots!* When you draw the lines outside of the limits of the nine dots this task is easy to accomplish. Reread the first paragraph and instructions. Who said that you could not draw a line that went outside of the dots? Hmmmm? Not I, says me. It was your own doing. You limited yourself to staying inside the nine dots, not the rules or the instructions.

As in the nine-dots challenge, you absolutely have to challenge all of your own limitations. You will find that you were never actually as limited as things appeared. In school you were taught that the scientific method starts with questions. Later, when you actually began to question things, you were probably abruptly scolded (like I was a time or three), and taught not to question the academic authority of professors and teachers.

Humor me in this: It's like being schooled on investment planning, financial management, and bookkeeping but being told to rely on a financial planner to choose your investments for you.

Here's a funny question: Does your financial planner and advisor actually buy for themselves what they are selling? Or do they actually invest in other things that you don't know about? Here's the funny answer: Perhaps some of them recommend things to you that provide an acceptable but limited return so they can make a commission selling to you, while they toy with the real investments that produce phenomenal returns. I always love to ask and find out what they really buy in their personal portfolios compared to what they offer me.

To bring this point home, I will tell you about a friend who is a licensed financial planner. I asked him what he could produce for someone entering his company with some cash. He gave a figure at that time of up to a possible 12% return. I told him that was way too poor of a return for me and that I looked for opportunities that provided at least a 100% return. At that point I had his attention while I endeavored to tell him how I found my opportunities. After listening awhile, he chuckled a little and then took me to his other computer screen and showed me how he was achieving a 300% return on his money! Boy was I humbled. I thought I really had one over on him, but found out that I was limiting myself to a mere 100% return by being so audacious as to think I was really doing something special.

Don't just buy what they sell; buy what they buy!

The New Economy

Thinking outside the dots will challenge old-school thinking and dogma. Remember the old philosophy of *"you have to get a good education to get a good job"* that was taught to our parents? This exhortation does not hold true in our new economy. We now live in an era of dot-commers, e-commerce, day-traders, and MLMers who have permanently changed the demographic face of the modern big money earners.

When I was young, I recall being schooled and instructed time and time again that I needed to graduate high school and then go on to college for an education as the only sure way to earn good money. Hogwash I say! That may have been true in the 40s and 50s and 60s, but it is an urban legend today. I am not saying to refuse an education and just survive the best way that you can. I am saying that the fortunes of today are not usually based in academic achievement, but are steeped in opportunities that were not even available a few short years ago.

To be perfectly clear: I'm not against getting an education— I'm actually all for it. Educational depth can add wonderful dimensions to life's experience. This I do say: *Educate for the sake of education and not necessarily for the sake of money earning potential.*

We as humans need to work at what we want to work at. We should work at what we like and like what we do above any other career choice. Measure it this way: Your personal success at a career should absolutely be measured by other means than financial increments. If someone wants to be a librarian, they ought to be one. And they should very well be the best librarian the world has ever seen. But they should do so because that is what they really want to do and not because that is their educational skill level and only means of providing finances for survival. What if your education is in library science but you soon find out that you absolutely hate library management? Should you acquiesce or should you explore other options outside the nine dots of library?

By the way, speaking of thinking outside the nine dots,

did you know that *linear income sucks?*

Linear income is this: You work an hour and you get paid an hour's wages. If you don't work an hour, you just simply don't get paid for that hour. With linear income, if you need a day off for a personal emergency, you have to check with your boss first so you do not get fired for taking off. If your boss does not deem your emergency as dire enough to warrant time off, then you have to suck rocks. Or worse yet, you can have the time off, but will suffer financial setbacks because of your absence and lack of pay. Time often equates to money, but not if you are working for the enjoyment of what you do. If you are going to spend time working for money, make it something you love to do. Never work for money—have money work for you.

How do you like them nine dots?

18 ♦ The Win-Win Situation

The eighteenth rule of holes:

It's only a good deal when both parties win

The BIL (Brother-in-law) prosperity

A good deal happens when both parties win. A compromise is where one or both parties are not necessarily happy and perhaps only one of them got a good deal.

On this note, I would like to discuss *the BIL prosperity*. Now, everyone loves a good deal, a break, a good-ole brother-in-law discount once in a while. And perhaps, just maybe the ole-BIL really simply wants to bless you with a good deal.

The questions for *the BIL prosperity* are as follows: 1. Do you want your BIL to prosper in his business? 2. Are you taking personal advantage of the BIL deal? 3. Would you get a better service/product if you paid the BIL full price? 4. Is this "discount" going to cause bad feelings within the family? 5. Quid-pro-quo (Is there going to be a "payback" required later and are you prepared to pay the piper when he comes calling?)

So many questions!

The answer to 1 has to be an unequivocal and resounding

YES. I want my BIL to prosper. In this case, offer to pay full price and if he is really simply wanting to bless you with a good deal, then accept it graciously and let him give *(after all it is more blessed to give than receive—let the BIL have his blessing)*.

The answer to 2 had better be a "No"! Keep in mind that it is okay to take a gift, but not if it is solely for personal gain at the expense of someone else (Refer back to number 1).

The answer to 3 is a tricky one. If it is quality that you need and the quality you expect isn't tendered, you lose. If you really don't care about quality and pay for less than perfection, you got what you paid for so don't feel bad about it later. Finally, IMO, if the BIL does an excellent job, offer to pay him the real value and let him decide to give with all his heart—or not.

The answer to 4 is a no-brainer. Keep peace in the family. Dissention and hurt is never worth the price in money. Remember, one of my personal philosophies is this: *People are to be loved and things are to be used. If you love things you will use people.*

The answer to number 5 belongs in a *Godfather* movie. Enough said?

The MLM (multi-level-marketing) factor

Is MLM a good deal for both parties? Let's start by looking at the MLM success and drop-out rates according to researcher Jon M. Taylor, PhD. In the first year, about 50% of MLM representatives drop-out—after paying in at entry level with who-knows-how-much money. After five years 90% have left the company. By year 10 over 95% have dropped out and only those at the top remain[14].

Starting into an MLM is always both very costly and very time consuming—requiring front-end purchase commitments, expensive "training materials", and specific levels of income or recruitment achievements to even start qualifying for compensation plans. Taylor's 2008 case study goes on to say that the number of people achieving top-level earnings was a meager 0.14% and a whopping 99.71% of participants lose money in an MLM (not even considering valuable time invested). The cherry on top of this pyramid-pie is that only 1 in 545 actually show *any* profit at all after expenses. Does this sound like a win-win?

Many mediocre MLMers explain their apparent and impending MLM failure with the explanation that *"I only got involved to help reduce the cost of this myriad of products I now order with auto-ship"*. But, in order to maintain the discounted goods, you still have to help capture more of your kind to the MLM machine.

Okay, I'm definitely not a fan of MLMs obviously, and if you

[14] Lilyquist, Mindy. "Multi-Level Marketing (MLM) Success Rates and Techniques." *The Balance Small Business*, The Balance Small Business, 29 Oct. 2018, www.thebalancesmb.com/the-likelihood-of-mlm-success-1794500. (Accessed online February 23, 2019).

happen to be one of the winning 0.29% (about 1/4 of 1%) then congratulations—I think. Just remember the fallen 99.71% who have failed to prosper in the MLM dream. *It has to be a good deal for all.*

Getting rich quick: How to catch a monkey

Sometimes good deals are one-sided monkey traps, only you are the monkey. This is especially true of virtually every get-rich-quick scheme ever. Get rich quick schemes are monkey traps that always make the schemer rich quick and not the schemee.

How to Catch a Monkey: To catch a monkey is actually a very simple task. All you need is a narrow neck bottle and a small banana. You stuff the banana in the bottle and tie the bottle to a tree limb where the monkey can see it. The monkey will spy the banana (object of desire) and reach into the bottle and firmly grasp the banana. The banana and the clenched fist will not, however, exit the bottle together and the monkey is now effectively trapped by his own greed and absolutely will not relinquish his grasp on the coveted banana. When the hunter comes to check his trap and glean his prize, the monkey will bare his teeth and fight with one hand and two feet, but still will refuse to relinquish the grip on the chosen spoils from the other hand, thus becoming effectively bourn to captivity for the rest of his life (not a good deal for the monkey).

Even though the little monkey gave a good fight, his greed was his downfall.

Keep in mind that a banana is actually a wonderful thing for any monkey to have, just not *that* banana at *that* particular time. The problem with monkey traps is that they look sooooo good and wonderful to the senses but are sooooo confining and uncomfortable when we become entangled by them. The other problem with traps is that they are sooooo easy to fall into. So easy in fact that it might behoove you to think twice when you find a carrot dangling in some convenient but unlikely place, looking so luscious and so accessible. In fact, if the situation looks to be too easy, it might bear a little research. If you do somehow fall for the proverbial monkey trap, you need to be wise enough to let go of the banana. It is **always** our own desires that keep us in some kind of captivity such as a one-sided deal. You may have heard it said: If it is too good to be true, it is probably just that, too good to be true!

A blind sow might find an acorn once in a while,
but keep in mind that if you want to catch a blind sow,
you might use an acorn to entice it to your lair.

Golden rule

The golden rule of thumb is to never take unfair advantage of anyone, even if you are just "passing it on" because you were taken advantage of. Win-win should conclude all of our deals. The deal has to be good for all concerned or someone gets hurt. I'm not talking about reaping where someone else sowed a crop and then gave up or failed to make it through to harvest time. I'm talking about out and out cheating someone. If someone loses a house because they were in a debt hole and could not make the payments and now you bought it at a discount, that is honest. But if you knowingly sell someone a bill of goods, a pig in a poke, ocean front property in Nebraska, that is what I call criminal.

Good morals are still available to those who wish to apply them.

19 ♦ All Assets are not Expendable

The nineteenth rule of holes:

Don't work for money, have money work for you

I wish to open this chapter by clarifying first a distinct difference in investments, because your home and your car are technically not investments.

Asset or liability?

A home and a car are not really expendable investments. They may be things that you insist on calling investments because you spend money on them, but they are technically not very good for listing on the asset side of the balance sheet. If you list them on the asset side, are you also willing to forfeit them as part of your investment portfolio? While you can leverage your home for investment capital, what happens if the venture investment you bought into doesn't pay out like you had hoped it would? Are you willing to "bet the farm" so to speak?

Let me approach this from another angle by asking you these questions: What is your biggest investment (pause here while you consider your answer)? Okay then, what is your second biggest investment? If you said your house for number one and your car for number two, you are in trouble already unless the house is a fixer upper that you will sell in the short term and your car is a bargain classic that you intend to sell for cash in the near future.

Unfortunately for most families, the two biggest investments they have in this life are their personal home and their family automobile. Neither of these are readily disposable for raising cash. So, are they really investments? Or are they necessities? Can you sell your home and live in your car? Is your vehicle technically a consumable good of sorts? Perhaps, even worse, the family vehicle is just a pretty bauble that is worth less today than what you gave for it yesterday.

Think about it like this, does your car go on the asset side of your ledger? Well... yeah. Okay then, does your car bring in monthly income? Well... no. Your car expenses always fall onto the expense side of the ledger with recurring monthly payments, maintenance, fuel, taxes, and insurance. The asset value of your car will also normally depreciate, sometimes very rapidly.

Okay, now for your home. While it is an investment technically, because you live in it, the home still costs you on the expense side of the ledger. Payments, taxes, maintenance, improvements, all come to my mind. Even worse than that, if you have the home financed on a 30-year mortgage, it will cost you

116

twice its original purchase price OR MORE by the time you pay it off. How about if you have an interest only loan? You never pay down the value of one of those loans, but rather "rent" the money you used to "buy" the home. The bank actually owns the asset and you just control the asset a little when you pay the money rent.

Did you know that a vast majority of millionaires do not own the house they live in? Some of these millionaires live next door to "the common folks" and live remarkably ordinary lives.

So, your home is not as easy to liquidate as stocks, bonds, coins, art, or other assets. You will always need a place to live, sleep, and take a shower. Therefore, your home really isn't an investment that helps provide immediate or short-term cash returns. If you needed quick cash you probably wouldn't dream of selling your house, would you? The expense of selling your home makes another debt when you buy the next home (plus closing costs, moving costs, financing fees, utility transfers, taxes and etc). In the end, you will always need a roof over your head and I daresay your mortgage payment and home-related expenses are actually recurring expenses.

True investments

True investments are liquid and impersonal. They can be

bought and sold pretty much at will. If your true investment pays off with a return, then rejoice, lather, rinse, repeat. If your true investment bombs, be sad for a few seconds and then move on. My best advice is to never risk more on an investment than you are comfortable losing. Then find different investment avenues in case one or more of them fail.

The best allegory for investing I can come up with is having a money pond fed with many streams of income.

True investments look for either short term or long term returns on investment. True investments, in my opinion, should never be bought with emotional attachments or executed under pressure. Careful investors research carefully while most high risk-takers jump in and out of investments, sometimes daily. The flavor of your personal investing style is not mine to judge, but let the records show what the return actually is, and then you can repeat what works and avoid what doesn't work.

Residual income

Residual income is what I call "mailbox money". This is my favorite income of all incomes. You invest in something, perhaps only once, and the only thing you have to do after that is walk to the mailbox to collect the check once a month. Some prime examples of residual income are recurring discretionary income, royalties, dividends, interest, and rent. Residual income is perhaps the most elusive of all money streams, but also perhaps the most satisfying of them all. Seeing as this book is not about personal investment advice, I will leave the research and development of your personal residual income up to you.

It was John D. Rockefeller who said:

"I would rather earn 1% off of 100 people's efforts than 100% of my own efforts."[15]

The emergency fund asset

While true investments are liquid and impersonal, I wouldn't count a family heirloom as either liquid or impersonal unless you fully intend to sell it anyhow. However, if you are holding on to it "in case of emergency", then it is actually a sort of savings account rather than a true investment asset—and that's okay too. Keep in mind that CNBC reported in 2018 that fewer than 34% of Americans could cover a $1,000 emergency with cash on hand and a whopping 55 million Americans had absolutely no savings at all. Are you one of these?

---

[15] "John D. Rockefeller Quotes." *BrainyQuote*, Xplore, www.brainyquote.com/quotes/john_d_rockefeller_165070. (Accessed online February 24, 2019).

Failing to plan

Coming to the end of this little chat about investments, I'll tell you a story about a friend of mine. In the mid 1960's, as a lad, my friend had this thought that somehow gold was going to be the investment that would eventually make him rich. The price of gold then was around $40 an ounce. I remember him buying one-1oz coin every other week by working odd jobs. Any chance he got he bought an extra coin or two. Even though the price of gold reached $160 an ounce by 1976, he remained faithful to his plan, setting aside $80 a week or more for his gold purchase. You'd have thought he was a miserly nut as he kept buying at least a coin or two every month. In 2011 I saw him stroll into a gold exchange company carrying just one of many PVC tubes of coins so heavy that he literally rolled it in on a small dolly. He cashed in 100, 1-oz coins, at over $1500 per ounce and then paid cash for a new home for his family.

Now I don't know just how many rolls of 100 coins this man had or even still has, but I certainly wish I had followed his example early on. Maybe right now you can only afford to buy 1 silver coin a week, or perhaps 2 shares of Caterpillar stock a month, but if you don't do something, you'll receive nothing. I'm not concerned at all with *what* you invest in, I want to know *that* you invest in something—and "Mattress National Bank" pays absolutely no dividends, so merely socking cash away (although perhaps a good idea also) will not increase your earnings.

I can sum this up this chapter by saying *"Don't work for money, have money work for you!"*

20 ♦ Destroyed by Good Things

The twentieth rule of holes:

Good isn't always best

Good, better, and best

There will always be choices in life, some easy and some difficult; some good, some bad. Bad choices aside for the moment, the thing about choices is that most of them are almost always a choice between good, better, and best. And here lies the main rub: Committing to a good choice could bind you from making a better choice. For instance: Marriage is a good thing in my opinion, but the timing of nuptials could result in a better decision if there is college to be completed or financial obligations that could be dealt with prior to the ceremony.

Needing to upgrade vehicles is another example. A good choice could be a brand spanking new car. A better choice might be a *newsed* car (slightly used car that is like new) that has already suffered the initial depreciation; or maybe even the best decision would be a completely paid for used car that will not depreciate much at all and save lots of money for the family budget.

122

Work or family

Perhaps one of the most difficult choices anyone can face is between work and family. You have to work to provide for the family—that's a good choice. But sometimes the amount of work to make ends meet cuts severely into family time. If and when there is family time for the overworked, it is often tainted with tiredness and attitude carried over from work.

The choice in this case isn't necessarily between good and bad, better and best, it is a choice of values. Which do you cherish more, family or career? What you value more is where you will invest in this case. If you value the "better" lifestyle your job affords the family over time spent with the family, well…you tell me. The good-better-best choice in this case may be one of choosing a smaller home, older car, and fewer things while you find new and different ways to invest your hard-earned assets rather than spending the money on the lifestyle upgrade.

Lee Iacocca once said: "No man on his death bed ever looked up into the eyes
of his family
and friends and said, "I wish I'd spent more time at the office."[16]

~~Some people have both the~~ great job and the upgraded lifestyle

[16] Barnes, Bob, and Emilie Barnes. *15 Minute Devotions for Couples*. Harvest House Pub, 2005. (P. 251)

while others struggle to pretend to have it all. Still others skip the upgrades and simply enjoy their families, hobbies, and spare time. At the end of your life will people say, "they sure worked hard and built that business career", or will they say "they sure loved their family"? Will they call you an overworked sourpuss or a relaxed happy person? You can choose which is best for you.

The comedy of errors

I mentioned earlier in this book that a classic writer, named Voltaire, wrote the wonderful short story named Candide. I was forced to read this story as a college class assignment leveled upon me by a history professor. I have never been an avid reader of "the classics" in literature, but I strongly recommend this book to all who aspire to make *best* choices in life. But please, go ahead and finish this book first! You are almost to the end! Then enjoy the satirical tale about this man, Candide, and his company of acquaintances. Regale in all of their adventures in life, and most especially the final summary of all the happenings at the very end.

It seems that this Candide fellow is always making from marginally good to obviously poor choices as he is immersed in sudden wealth. You will find a lot of humor in the good-but-not-best philosophies of the sages that Candide sought for advice. Contradictions abound as Candide applies various templates to his own thinking and allows pride to blind him to the facts until

124

the very end. The most amazing part of this classic is some of the life-truths behind money and huge financial gain that Candide stumbled through. You will experience his various choices and attitudes and perhaps even feel in your heart, his heart toward money, fame, and philosophy.

In the end, you can reflect, as I did, over the acquisition of wealth and the challenges it brings with it. You can sneer and shake your head as I did at the vain ramblings of the "wise" men. And you can shudder at the immoral advantages that the merchants, traders, and scoundrels took of Candide's treasure. But most of all you can learn a little about wealth and philosophy and reflect upon the misadventures and plan your own escape to them if these misadventures happen to you.

Laws of wisdom

I'm certain everyone has heard the old adage attributed to Albert Einstein: *"The definition of insanity is doing the same thing over and over again, but expecting different results."*

Perhaps you can recall in the very beginning of this book I said:

> To pay the price for your financial education in life three choices exist:
>
> 1   Study at the feet of successful teachers and mentors
> 2   Watch and heed the mistakes and successes of

others

3 Make all your own mistakes and pay your own tuition

Wisdom is knowledge applied and knowledge often comes at a price. Here's the thing. If you make a bad decision—or even a series of life-clogging *good* decisions, embrace the lesson and apply the wisdom—don't repeat the mistake. You should only have to pay tuition for financial and other life's lessons once and once only *if you can learn to apply the laws of wisdom*. Wisdom will keep you from repeating historical errors by doing the same things twice or more and reaping the same bad result. Even if the fault isn't your own: *Fool me once, shame on you. Fool me twice, shame on me.*

◆ Conclusion ◆

Wow, did you really just finish reading this book? As you turn the final page, I wish to convey my heart in writing this book about my experiences to you, the reader. I know that experience is no guarantee for truth, but experience is one awesome teacher when tempered by truth. In the end, does my book impact your life? Does it cause some fundamental yet profound change in your heart? I truly hope it does.

With this in mind, I thank you profusely for taking valuable time out of your busy life to read and hopefully glean something meaningful and useful out of this book. ~ **The end**

Made in the USA
Monee, IL
23 December 2023